ENDLESS
SEA

Alone Around Antarctica—as Far South as a Boat Can Sail

ENDLESS SEA

AMYR KLINK

Translated by Thomas H. Norton

SHERIDAN HOUSE

First published 2008
in the United States of America by
Sheridan House, Inc.
145 Palisade Street
Dobbs Ferry, NY 10522
www.sheridanhouse.com

First published in Brazil under the title
Mar Sem Fim: 360° ao redor da Antártica
by Editora Schwarcz Ltd. São Paulo

Library of Congress Cataloging-in-Publication Data

Klink, Amyr
    [Mar sem fim. English]
    Endless sea : alone around Antarctica—as far South as a boat can sail /
Amyr Klink ; translated by Thomas H. Norton.
        p. cm.
    ISBN 978-1-57409-259-2 (pbk. : alk. paper)
    1. Klink, Amyr—Travel—Antarctica. 2. Paratii (Ship) 3. Antarctica—
Description and travel. I. Title.
    G585.K55A313 2008
    910.9167—dc22
    [B]
                                                                    2008007335

Photos by Amyr Klink
Maps and line drawings by Sirio Cançado
Edited by Janine Simon
Designed by Keata Brewer

Printed in the United States of America

ISBN 918 1 57409 259 2

E ao imenso e possível oceano
Ensinam esta Quinas, que aqui vês,
Que o mar com fim sera grego ou romano:
O mar sem fim é português.

As to the vast and possible ocean
Tell these escutcheons you see
That the bounded sea may be Greek or Roman:
The endless sea is Portuguese.

Fernando Pessoa,
Mensagem, "Padrão", September 13, 1918

CONTENTS

1

SWEEPING
THE DUST

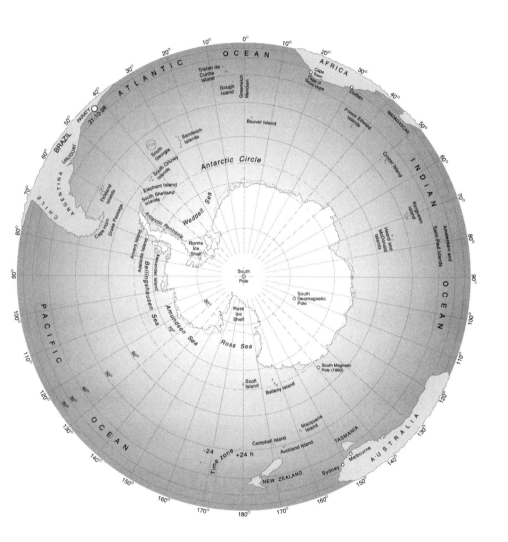

The twins are busy digging in the sand, little white bonnets bobbing on their heads at the water's edge in Jurumirim. With pails, brightly colored shovels and cookie-cutter molds, they are building and demolishing castles in the sand.

I am leaving soon. In a few short hours I will know months of separation, of a kind I've never experienced before. For the moment, however, on board PARATII, from where I watch my daughters, we have run into more problems.

I should have been long gone by now, but our first shakedown cruise from Santos to Paraty had exposed a problem. To fix it, we decided to replace the original mainsail batten screws with nuts and bolts. This was a minor but annoying detail. Why not just trust British engineering and its fine manufacturer? Why not leave things as they were? What difference could such tiny parts—dead-ended screws versus bolts with nuts—make on such a long voyage?

I wasn't sure what difference they might make, but I knew that in a 100-mile shakedown cruise under fair-weather conditions, two batten cars had come apart. This certainly didn't make me happy. With a voyage of 18,000 hard-driven miles ahead, and five long months far from any sign of civilization, it seemed wisest not to rely on manufacturers; so now we will tighten a nut onto every bolt.

One more orange dinghy ride over to the town pier. One more drive up the mountain to São Paulo looking for the simple parts that are impossible to find in the small town of Paraty. One more item added to the never-ending check list. Patience, patience.

This time, it was Luís who drove off to locate the tiny nuts we needed. Hermann stayed with me to handle the back-up main-

Jurumirim. The twins on the beach

sail. It was so heavy we decided to tow it over to the beach where the coconut trees could provide shade while we replaced the batten car screws.

The two little girls on the beach barely notice the odd, long rolls of sails passing alongside their castles and disappearing into the trees. They just keep digging—these two most precious creatures on earth.

Marina sets the lunch table—consisting of baby bottles—on a wooden bench nearby, under a large mango tree that dips down so far it almost touches the smooth, crystalline water at high tide. It is hot; not a hint of wind. I know this calm will soon come to an end, and also my nervousness.

There is nothing joyful about departures, saying goodbye is sad, but to some extent, I am already gone. The earth underfoot now seems vaguely unstable, I already miss those still here with me. A strange, urgent yearning draws me toward my first gale, the sighting of the first albatross, the first wandering icebergs. It is a yearning to finally set my boat free to run the giant waves of the Antarctic Convergence.

We spent our last night together in the little house on Jurumirim Bay, blowing out the kerosene lamps while it was still early. The next morning, a brief stopover at PARATII so the twins can roam her decks one last time, and then Marina and the girls board the whaler SOL DE VERÃO, for the ride out of this tiny bay and over to the town pier.

It's better this way, with no farewells, no words. I hug each of them tightly. As they head off, I wave nervously. I make a silent wish to see them again, perhaps around the autumnal equinox, when the twins will turn two.

Departing Brazil in October, with provisions for six months, I plan to spend an entire summer at sea in latitudes where the sun barely disappears at nighttime. If the sails and route are handled correctly (and nothing goes wrong), perhaps I can make it back by March 25 of next year, to kiss the fair and dark heads of my twin beauties.

The whaler turns out of Jurumirim Bay and slips from view. For a few seconds time stands still.

On board, back to the mad rush. Lying at anchor, off the bow toward the beach, is another red sailboat, CASO SÉRIO. She looks a lot like PARATII and was built by the same designer, Cabinho, though she is much smaller, almost minuscule. She serves as the permanent home to my friend, Sérgio, a Varig Airlines pilot. Sérgio has discreetly been watching his boat's older (and equally crimson) sister, keeping an eye on all the activities as she prepared for her departure. I shanghaied him to help me make some final adjustments. He lends me a book by Bernard Moitessier and a little witch doll, which I tie with a ribbon to the column in the saloon. As a gift, he hands me a small wrapped can that I am not supposed to open until Christmas, eight weeks from now.

Saturday morning, rain. I hoist the sails—at last they are ready—and slip the mooring line in Jurumirim. "Take care, Amyr," Hermann embraces me awkwardly. He jumps into the orange dinghy with Álvaro, Sérgio, and my Portuguese friends, João and Paulo. These five, the only eyewitnesses to my departure, accompany me from a distance through relentless rain out to the mouth of the bay. I've always loved the rain in Paraty; it makes the waters greener and sharpens the colors of the mountain forests surrounding the bay. Jurumirim, a bay within a bay, soon slips from view.

Next to disappear astern are the church steeples and the towering palm trees of the town, deep within the greater bay. Far away, Hermann raises his arm high. My five friends are gone. I wave as I head off. I wipe my rain-soaked face with the sleeve of my red jacket, which doesn't taste salty—not yet. A scream comes from deep within me, incomprehensible. It is a long shout of joy, of relief.

I should have been nervous. I am underway on my first-ever voyage around the world. I have chosen a difficult route—the most difficult route one could choose. I know there is a high probability that I will be unable to complete the voyage. I could be forced to quit—by a breakdown, exhaustion, or some error—just as so many have before me. I am well aware that over the next five months I will be facing the roughest, most temperamental and ice-ridden seas in the world, with no one to turn to for help.

This will be no mere crossing of that stretch of huge waves that roll unhindered around Antarctica. No, I am to become a long-term resident of those waves. Night and day will be spent negotiating strong winds, angry seas, fog, snow flurries, and iceberg traffic. This voyage will take me far beyond the Roaring Forties or the Furious Fifties, sometimes even into the "silent latitudes," where winds that elsewhere scream and groan, simply grow mute.

Sailors of old called it "beyond hell." The high latitudes have many folkloric names that are pretty unnerving. Also worrisome, because of their frequency, are the records of catastrophic weather, cold, and rogue waves. Yet the fact is, despite the power of these phenomena of the Southern Ocean, much has been exaggerated. The countless stories of dramatic experiences down there often have more to do with a lack of common sense and planning than about ice, waves, or wind. Many of those stories tell of futile heroism and false adventure. They are the accounts of hollow bravery displayed by people who failed to pay due respect to the Polar Regions.

A good number of those stories are traveling with me, stowed in PARATII's lockers. But I also brought along other writings, stories of true courage and boldness demonstrated by men who understood how to negotiate the challenges and the fear, competent pioneers who forged new routes, discovered uncharted corners of the world—and made it back home.

It's true, I should be nervous after so many months of contingency planning and preparations. After all, I am setting out on a voyage bigger and more difficult than any I have ever undertaken. But I am not nervous. As the last shadows of Joatinga Point with its two remaining coconut trees drop away astern, I feel a quiet confidence. From this point forward, for the first time, any problems and any potential incidents will be delivered to a single address, on board PARATII.

Once all the housecleaning is finished, and all lines and fenders are secured, I lash the painted broom inside the forepeak locker, next to a pair of fine wooden oars typically used by the fishermen from Paraty. It is Saturday, October 31—Halloween and I haven't even noticed. With my witch doll and broom aboard, I drop south under full sail, at long last distancing myself from the infinite calm of Jurumirim.

I have just taken a broom to the worst dust of all—the dust that settles on sailors and boats that never leave port.

2

THE DEAD ISLAND

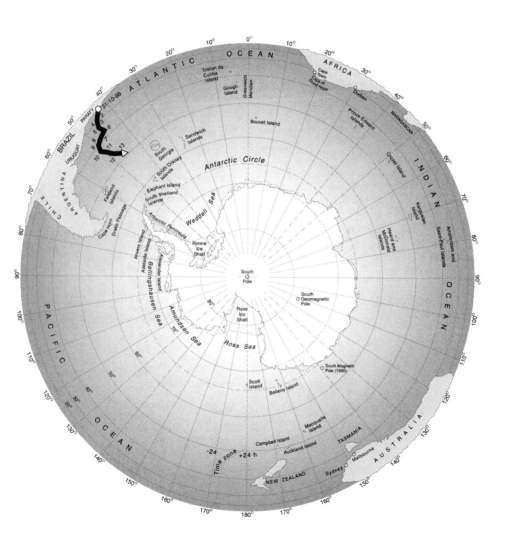

After nine years of living with PARATII I had come to admire the durability and strength of her 50-foot aluminum hull, and to know every detail about her, inch by inch. My greatest worry was the new Aerorig mast overhead, speared into the deck and rising 80 feet into the air, unstayed and with no controlling lines other than a blue mainsheet. It was white, a free-standing, 360-degree-rotating mast, the sole supporting element to PARATII's sails; a bold and highly controversial feat of technology. I had chosen to place my trust in it.

The idea of this mast had stirred up quite a bit of chatter among sailors. The brilliant man who brought the invention to life, Damon Roberts, got the idea from a toy boat called a *marblehead*, which has only two controls, one for the rudder and one for the sails—and an unstayed mast. Roberts had managed to dodge the apathy that can so easily choke creativity. So often, in our zeal to find sophisticated solutions we bypass brilliantly simple alternatives. His was a revolutionary idea, incredibly simple and efficient.

Roberts, the English genius, was married to a Brazilian from the state of Minas Gerais and spoke Portuguese. His delays in building the mast, so uncharacteristic of the British, almost drove me mad. It caused us to completely miss our original departure date. The voyage had been postponed for one unbearably miserable year. PARATII's old mast had already been taken down. A massive restructuring had been completed, which included ripping up and re-welding the deck in preparation for the new mast. Yet the new mast itself was nowhere in sight.

With the voyage postponed by a year, I managed to convince Roberts to make some changes to the design of the main section of the rig. The original design was cylindrical and vertically straight. Now, I wanted the mast to be wing-shaped, with aerodynamic curves. I also wanted it pre-bent, or raked, to allow for greater headsail tension.

I heard every imaginable sort of comment from folks who thought I was making a mistake by putting my trust in this new mast. They claimed it was too unconventional and unreliable, muttering that it was too risky to take chances on an unproven design when facing the rigors of a Southern Ocean circumnavigation.

The funny thing was, the more I heard the idea disparaged, the more I fell in love with it. Though I liked the elegance of the design—an inverted cross supported at two points, the deck and the keel—what fascinated me most was the solidity this mast conveyed, with its tremendous height and flexibility. No similar mast had ever completed a circumnavigation, either cruising or racing—not even along the easier tropical routes. Most experts had never even laid eyes on one of these carbon crosses. The few who were acquainted with it believed in its miraculous qualities the same way one would trust an elixir of youth. To me, the new mast had come to mean exactly that. It was indeed a magical solution.

The conditions I would face during the months ahead would be rough, very rough. In fact, that was the secret dream I had been nurturing for so long. I wanted to feel the hull of my big red truck rumbling down Southern Ocean waves for days and weeks on end. Having sailed PARATII for years, I knew well that the secret to building a seaworthy boat lies not in the use of heavy-duty materials, but rather in the simplicity of design and solutions. I had an aversion to complex control systems. Handling a conventional rig while surfing down large waves in following seas was

PARATII with her new mast.

Getting under way

simply too time-consuming and risky. There was no need for senseless hardship or risks.

On PARATII handling sails while sailing upwind had always been comfortable and simple, but in a strong following wind it was easy to make mistakes. One mistake and she could broach or even end her career in a beautiful capsize. I had considered installing dual headstays in order to fly double jibs downwind. Singlehanded sailors in the past had often turned to this simple solution, but I was not convinced it was the best one.

One day while reading a magazine in Chile I ran across an article about Damon's system, which had been patented by Carbospars. After months of begging and insisting, I finally received an invitation to a sea trial in a boat rigged with one of these strange contraptions. Not many of these masts had crossed the Atlantic, so I traveled to Oban, Scotland. FLYER, a 78-foot sloop, had just completed an amazingly fast round-trip transatlantic crossing, crewed only by a charming couple in their 70s. That sea trial was a turning point in my plans.

Following that Scottish Highlands experience, I embarked on a new mission. I scrounged up every penny I could find and, burning the midnight oil, drew up a new rigging plan, and ordered the carbon monster. But all the work, the high price, and the bureaucratic hoop-jumping I did while planning for and purchasing the new mast would pale in comparison to the greater challenge still ahead: stepping the damn thing.

June arrived, and after eight months of delays and countless bureaucratic hassles, I finally slipped my hand inside the mast, still in its box, and rubbed the raw carbon fibers with my fingers. It was delivered to the port of Santos, to the same container terminal where I had received PARATII's former mast, nine years earlier. But this time the problems with stepping the mast were much larger. In size alone, it was 20 feet taller and much more delicate than its predecessor.

The shipping company, Hamburg-Süd, not only handled all the administrative aspects of the operation, but they generously made their ship's cranes available to raise and step the mast through PARATII's deck. Sadly, it proved an impossible task.

We wanted to avoid hauling the mast on a flatbed truck down an obstacle course of electrical wires and street corners, all the way over to Pier 26 in Guarujá, where PARATII had been made ready. So we decided to step the mast right there at the dock.

First, the boom had to be laid along the deck, followed by a sequence of precision steps—a coupling here, feeding a line there, and so forth. The base of the mast had to be manhandled through every step of the orchestrated movement. The slightest error at the crane controls could have meant the loss of fingers, hands, or even the mast itself.

The unit consisted of two parts, not just one. One part was the mast itself, 80 feet tall. The other part was the square-bodied boom, which was 42 feet long. In the center of the boom was a square opening. The mast would have to be threaded through that square opening and then through the deck to the keel, followed by dozens of electrical wires manually routed home, each to its own distinctive address. Once the mast had successfully been eased through the center square on the boom, the two parts of the rig would form an inverted cross. The next step would be to "spear" the mast through the opening in the deck, passing smoothly through its first load-bearing point, the deck, and nestling snugly onto the second load-bearing point, the keel.

The shipping terminal decided to let us use its main crane and one of the slips normally booked by large ships. But there was a catch: it was available for one day only, and not a minute beyond midnight. Unfortunately, when that day came the seas around the dock were choppy. At dockside, my friends Thierry, who was in charge of the "spearing" project, and Pilotto, were both on edge as they participated in the mast-raising effort. Fábio, whose soot-caked surgical garb still bore the stains of recent surgeries, making him look more like a dockside mechanic than the surgeon he was, hopped up and down as he watched restlessly.

Waves slapped against PARATII, causing her to roll. The night crept along, but the mast was still a long way from being stepped. To make things worse, the darkness now prevented us from communicating with gestures. Using radios, we instituted a two-stage relay system. A request that the crane operator, 130 feet above us, raise or lower the mast by a few inches this way or that, involved two stages of relayed instructions followed by two stages of relayed acknowledgement.

By 9:00 p.m., everyone was exhausted; the employees at the

terminal were becoming irritated. Fábio, an expert in tricky operations and an eternal optimist, insisted that we try one more time.

Suddenly, the boat stopped rocking, for thirty seconds—a virtual miracle. The immense post descended out of the sky, slipped through the opening in the boom, slid precisely into the rotating ring and, to the sound of our cheers, eased its way into its permanent home on the boat—with not an inch to spare.

As the mast foot settled into its slot on the keel it smashed a little Norwegian coin, an *öre* I had placed there. No one else even knew about it—a Norwegian tradition with which I decided not to quarrel. Using a flashlight I screwed the bolts into the foot of the mast, and that same night PARATII returned to Pier 26. Due to yet another unforgivable oversight of the British, the sails had not been shipped, so for three more weeks we all burned with curiosity, waiting to see the mast in action.

The first sea trial in Santos was a shock. I realized that I had in my hands a new and surprising boat, a spirited twenty-ton machine, responsive to the slightest movements of my fingers. Sail adjustments were instantaneous. The ease was startling. The helm became light as a feather; the course, perfectly balanced. Whether or not this contraption would withstand months of Southern Ocean blows or even a possible capsize, only time and experience would tell. But, deep down, I had no more doubts.

I spent the following months of sea trials chasing squalls, making abrupt maneuvers, over-canvassing, and stressing the mast as much as possible. Marcão, a veteran sailor, became an expert in "radical jibes." At times there would be ten or twelve of us, adults all, riding the boom like children, flying back and forth over the deck. While the twins drank from their baby bottles on the same deck that had once been covered with a mess of lines, I made full circles under full sail, with never more than three or four fingers lightly touching the helm.

There was nothing to doubt about this new rig's strength. And the boat looked pretty with this unusual cross grafted into the deck. Miles of lines and almost a ton of complicated hardware that had once cluttered the deck were now gone.

"Now that wasn't so great," I mumble, withdrawing into the safety of the pilothouse to avoid getting hosed by dark water. It is early, Monday morning and I have just gone through my first southwesterly gale—of course, in total darkness. But reducing sail has been an easy and dry affair. I did not even touch the autopilot. With the mainsail taken in to its last reef, our speed has not dropped at all. Standing there, I give myself a few seconds to savor the minor pleasure of having successfully handled another sail adjustment, and then I jump into bed to catch some precious sleep.

Three days into the voyage, I have already become accustomed to the work schedule I will try to stick to from now on. Thirty minutes of sleep for each hour of being awake. All told, that will mean five, maybe even six hours of sleep per day. What got me initially was not rousting myself out of bed after only a half-hour of sleep, but figuring out how to fall asleep as quickly as possible. PARATII is indifferent to my own personal problems with the new schedule on board, and she holds her course during those thirty minutes like a machine driven by its own will.

The winds are still indecisive and light. The autopilot is in charge of maintaining our heading. As soon as the wind firms up, I will transfer PARATII's steering over to the windvane. It is a Swedish self-steering system, elegantly engineered and simple, and it consumes not a drop of electricity.

Little by little, I am gaining latitude and distance from the coast of South America. I passed the southernmost point of Brazil, Chuí; then Uruguay. When I enter international waters, with Argentina far abeam, I will tackle the only remaining problem of the voyage.

It isn't exactly a problem, but more of a decision, a final decision about our route. In a sense, the voyage I planned is simple, easy to define and trace on a map: I will circle the globe around Antarctica. I will depart from one point on the chart and sail east continuously, until I make my way back to the starting point.

That is my plan—a plan possible only in this particular band of high latitudes, between 50°S and 65°S. I call these the free latitudes, because they are uninterrupted by continents, with only one strangulation point: Drake Passage, between Cape Horn and the Antarctic Peninsula. Drake Passage squeezes through latitudes 56°S and 63°S—only seven degrees of freedom. The route is well known for its horrible weather and dramatic shipwrecks, probably more than it should be, primarily because in the past shipping traffic was heavy in those waters.

Prior to the opening of the Panama Canal in 1914, world shipping between the Atlantic and the Pacific Oceans had no choice but to descend to these latitudes, a route punctuated by the well-known rocky dangers of Cape Horn. Once the Panama Canal opened, cargo ships stopped coming, but the area kept its fame.

The most important element of the Drake Passage is a line that runs through it. It is not an imaginary line, like the parallels of latitude or meridians of longitude, but rather a line that defines the Antarctic Convergence. The Antarctic Convergence is a precise line that wraps around the globe, a border separating the cold waters of the North from the frozen waters of Antarctica. It is a thermally visible line—a hull thermometer can locate it with ease.

Most of my voyage will take place south of this line—the entire region south of the Antarctic Convergence is called "The Antarctic," whereas the continent is referred to as "Antarctica."

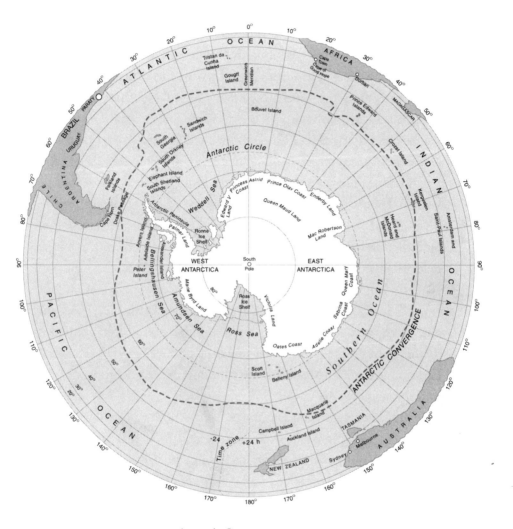

Antarctic Convergence map

I intend to start my polar circumnavigation at some point inside the Convergence, so in a sense I don't feel yet that I am quite underway.

The leg I sailed from Jurumirim down to the "cold line"—a long one, it's true—merely brought me toward my true starting point. I purposely chose not to identify it; not before I was certain that everything was running smoothly and that no unscheduled stopover would be necessary. I had yet to identify the precise spot—and get there.

Before leaving Brazil I thought of two possible departure points and landfalls along the way. The first landfall would be Dorian Bay. I had been there with PARATII several years earlier, iced-in for one year and seven days and I had always dreamed of a return visit. The second landfall would be Brazil's Comandante Ferraz station on King George Island, where I had first crewed on RAPA NUI, the beloved blue ketch that introduced me to the sailing life.

I had picked out the two departure points on British Admiralty Nautical Chart 3200: the Melchior Islands, an excellent gateway to the Antarctic Peninsula, and South Georgia, which is further east and a part of the Scotia underwater ridge. South Georgia is the star of all sub-Antarctic islands and I have not yet had the privilege to land there.

I still have a few days to make up my mind. Heading toward the Antarctic Peninsula—to the Melchior Islands—will mean cruising along the South American coast. If I run into any problems I should be able to make an emergency stopover in Patagonia or on the Falklands where resources are available, prior to crossing the Drake Passage. However, with that choice I will lose my first opportunity to visit the sub-Antarctic paradise of South Georgia.

I had been influenced by an impressive book I perused at Júlio's house in São Paulo, *Antarctic Oasis* by Tim and Pauline Carr. I am sorry I did not borrow it. I decided that day that I would set my course for South Georgia.

The authors of that uncommon book, after cruising all the oceans of the world in their small and charming 100-year-old sailboat, without an engine or a head, CURLEW, had fallen in love with South Georgia Island's icy and vibrant beauty. They dropped anchor there and for the past six years have lived aboard CURLEW. Perhaps they would still be there when I arrived.

"Must be quite a place," I thought.

So I pointed PARATII and her inverted cross toward the island. It was as simple as choosing an ice cream flavor.

As I tried to remember the book, which I had only leafed through that day long ago, what came to mind was the funny look on Fábio's face. Fabio had also fallen victim to the book. He pointed to the photograph of a snowy pristine anchorage and shouted: "This is it! This is where we must go, Amyr!"

I had completely forgotten that I had met the Carrs before, in Ilha Grande Bay. Ours would be a great reunion. Now heading for South Georgia Island, with South America falling farther and farther astern, I began to remove all other options from the table.

At the end of my first week at sea and the first thousand miles since leaving Jurumirim, I receive a gift, an unexpected surprise. Yesterday, I saw my first albatrosses, rare and surprising sightings. Today, petrels, fulmars, albatrosses and other, smaller birds appear in droves. This doesn't make sense to me. Up ahead, thousands of birds are circling and alighting on what seems to be an island or sandbar of some sort.

"This doesn't make sense," I think, grabbing my binoculars after double-checking the charts. We are 420 miles east of Mar del Plata and, as far as I know, there are no islands in this part of the Atlantic Ocean. But there it is, directly in front of me—a bird-infested rock. Short waves lap against it. The depth here is 5,300 meters, and the charts say nothing about land . . . could it be?

I disengage the autopilot and take the helm, steering into an approach. Yes, it is an island. A floating island . . . a dead island . . . a huge whale—bloated, afloat, and covered with so much life, so many birds that it is impossible to identify it as a dead whale. I make two more passes before continuing on toward my true island to the south.

As I ponder the now-deserted whaling factories I will find in South Georgia, I do not grieve for this whale's death. I wish all whales could die free like this one, now a floating island upon which birds and fish might feast, instead of being slaughtered like cattle.

3

A REAL ISLAND

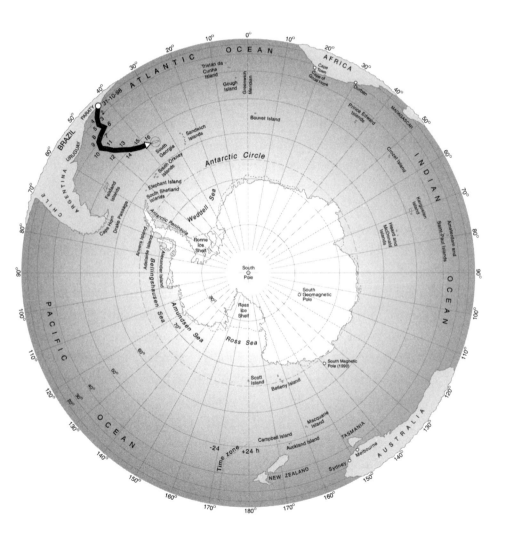

Lazy jacks are light and relatively unimportant lines that run from the top of the mast to fixed points on either side of the boom. Their purpose is to guide and secure the mainsail while it is being furled. A few days ago a mistake I made during a night-time jibe caused one of the lazy jacks to snap, and I was hell-bent on repairing it.

Several attempts to go aloft using a pseudo bosun's chair made out of mountain climbing gear made it painfully obvious that the jury-rigged contraption was incompatible with the halyards.

I rummaged for the umpteenth time on deck through my bag of mountain-climbing gear. This time, I found some ascenders used for climbing cave walls and assembled the makeshift bosun's chair. I strapped myself into the harness and began my ascent. When I had hauled myself up about 20 feet, I was suddenly thrown outward from the mast, away from the boat, and toward the sea. In a split second I found myself in midair, swooping over the waves. What a dreadful feeling! I longed for the company of a charitable soul who could lasso my feet and haul them back to "earth."

Though hanging from the heeling mast over the Atlantic Ocean while my boat sailed alongside was terrifying, I really had no other choice. The harness would have to work. I would have given anything for the mast steps from my previous mast, ancient and obsolete as they were. This was not a great moment to be-moan the fact that mast steps are unsuitable for carbon fiber masts. So I took a deep breath and resumed my climb.

*　　*　　*

Fifteen minutes later—and 60 feet higher—what a spectacular view of PARATII, way down there! And what violent motion up here! Instead of tying a knot—a task made virtually impossible because the mast was slamming back and forth so wildly—I anchored the lazy jack line with a tiny shackle and released the ascender. In seconds I was back down on the boom. Success!

In my euphoria, I couldn't wait until our next scheduled radio contact with ham operators in São Paulo. I had to call home now, so I took a chance and tried the Iridium phone.

I had brought along a small satellite telephone that was still being tested. The final model would be not be on the market until January, and the only way to get my hands on it would be to arrange for a landfall in some civilized corner on Antarctica. This little telephone was amazing. Marina answered and turned on the speakerphone. For the first time in my life I heard the words, "*Bom dia, Babai*!" Good morning, Daddy! The twins' noises came through the receiver as they jumped up and down and screamed giddily in the background.

As I listened to the tiny voices of my precious daughters, PARATII surfed, enjoying her first favorable winds. One big wave took her to fourteen knots, a new record. There I was, cruising in heavy seas, enjoying a dry deck, and fighting off a terrible bout of homesickness. I lost any notion of how many minutes I was on the phone, but it was a long time.

After the call, I redirected my remaining euphoria to a long-overdue operation of general hygiene. I bathed, cut my hair, and shaved my beard—all tasks were completed before nightfall.

Strangely enough, in the early hours of my thirteenth day at sea, the petrels and albatrosses which had been flying around us, skimming through the darkness just ahead of the waves—when not inspecting the boat's phosphorescent wake—simply vanished. Perhaps they knew the wind was also about to disappear.

*   *   *

The night is pitch-black. Any sense of the expanse of the surrounding seas is reduced to what little I can make out by the dim light of PARATII's phosphorescent wake. I begin to feel cold for the first time. I go below to grab a sweater. When I look out the starboard porthole, I am shocked to find an ice pack running close alongside and astern. It is a ghostly sight, unusually smooth-edged and low-lying. It looks like fast ice, a type of ice never seen at this latitude . . .

I switch on the hull thermometer. The water temperature has dropped by 42°F. Finally, I have reached the Antarctic Convergence. But ice? Here?

I spend a few minutes out in the cockpit trying to figure out how I could have stumbled upon an ice pack without waking up. Then it hits me. This is not ice at all, but an optical illusion. A thin coat of fog created by the difference between the air and the sea temperature. Reflected in the water, it looks like an ice pack that stretches as far as I can see.

Saturday, November 14, perhaps to commemorate our passing into the Antarctic Convergence . . . *POW!* A shot on deck. The boom instantly spuns into the wind and PARATII comes to a sudden stop. The heavy-duty pad eye for the mainsheet—which, by the way, is the only sheet on board—broke. Had this been a traditional rig, the boom would have broken too. Within minutes, and using nothing but line, I rig a new attachment point for the sheet—without using any mechanical fittings whatsoever.

We are underway again. This is agonizing in itself, not because of the cold—I am now donning gloves and a wool cap pulled down hard over my ears—but rather because of our heading. The wind is strong and on our nose, forcing the crew to spend the entire weekend tacking, drawing zigzags across the sea.

On one of those "zags" I discover that I am not the only mammal in this area. A full 206 miles from the nearest land, South Georgia Island, and over 1,000 miles from South America, a group of fur seals show up, racing the waves and spinning through the air in a display of total joy. They must be a few of the 2,000-plus fur seals that populate South Georgia Island—the largest community of its species on earth.

Earth! When will I see land?

Before long some piece of land should appear on the horizon, just ahead. Perhaps it will be Bird Island, or even the northern coast of South Georgia Island itself. I want to sleep but an array of entertaining sights keep me awake. Sheets of kelp are all around. I hope desperately that they won't foul the rudder. At daybreak, our first snow flurry. Snowflakes cover the deck and form small snowdrifts in the mainsail cover.

Just as I am wondering which vegetables I have on board that might serve as eyes and nose on a snowman, the party is over. The wind freshens, the snow stops falling, and the sun appears. In an instant, the entire horizon is transformed.

Land! Land ho!

It is imposing, and a thousand times more beautiful than in any photo I have ever seen. There are no clouds; just mountains and icebound peaks, black escarpments and large ice floes sparkling in the sunshine. I spend the day coasting along the northern side of the island.

At five o'clock in the afternoon, PARATII touches the wooden pier at Grytviken.

From the rubble of the old whaling station, a woman appears to take my lines and show me where to tie up.

"Welcome! Dinner will be served in a few minutes!" It is Pauline Carr.

For six years now, Tim and Pauline have been the only

permanent residents of South Georgia Island. When I first met them in Ilha Grande Bay, they were still flirting with the idea of living in this unique corner of paradise. I doubt than anyone else has ever stayed on South Georgia Island for that long a stretch, including the Norwegians who ran their whaling factories here for over fifty years.

Although the island was discovered by Antoine de La Roche in 1675, it was not until a century later that Captain James Cook set foot here, on his second and famous circumnavigation aboard RESOLUTION. For a long time the region would remain isolated and of little interest to explorers, had it not been for the publication of Cook's meticulous logs in 1774, in which he noted the abundance of seals and whales in this faraway place.

The Cook expedition, consisting of two ships, ADVENTURE and RESOLUTION, left England in 1772 for the sole purpose of trying to locate the continent of Antarctica. Though the existence of the continent was widely presumed, no one had been able to find it. Cook's ships circled Antarctica for three years and made countless other discoveries around the globe. Other than signs of fierce stresses at work in the ocean ice, Cook never saw any solid evidence of the continent. In the end, he concluded that the Antarctic continent must not exist after all.

The whalers and sealers of the day, much better prepared and more daring than any nation-sponsored exploring ventures, took a serious interest in Cook's logs. Though the scientific establishment and the navies did not show much interest in Cook's expeditions, they did produce a windfall—measured in blubber and skins. A new age of heavy hunting was born. The first hunts targeted fur seals and southern elephant seals. In 1905, attention turned to whales.

The island, which Cook named in an uninspired moment, is indeed a special place. It has no direct volcanic origins, as do most of the ocean islands in the Antarctic, though the vestiges of volcanoes are everywhere. It is the largest portion of exposed land in the Scotia Island arc, also known as the Scotia Ridge, a mountain range that forms the geographical link between the Andes and the Antarctic Peninsula. This range also includes the Burdwood Bank, Shag Rocks, the South Sandwich, South Orkney, and South Shetland Islands, where most Antarctic bases were established. Surrounded by these outcroppings of the Scotia Island arc, with depths up to 4,500 meters, is the Scotia Sea, which reaches into the Atlantic like an appendix extending from the Pacific Ocean as far as the Sandwich Islands.

South Georgia Island is surrounded by nonstop iceberg traffic as they make their exodus from the Weddell Sea, journeying toward their ultimate meltdown. The island boasts its own spectacular ice production, with over 150 glaciers of its own. Mountain climbers love this place and often venture into its hidden bays in search of virgin climbs. The island has almost three hundred peaks that range from 700 to 3,000 meters in altitude. Most have never been climbed or even named.

Of all the island's special qualities, however, the most notable is its exuberant wildlife. The densest Antarctic and sub-Antarctic wildlife makes its home on this remote piece of land, only 100 miles long and 20 miles wide. The world's largest population of wandering albatrosses; over 90 percent of the world's fur seal population; over half of all existing elephant seals; a third of all Papua penguins (the same species that had witnessed my winter beset by ice on Dorian Bay); and 800,000 King penguins—perhaps the most beautiful bird of the species. Despite cycles of exploitation that almost exterminated the seals and elephant seals, the wildlife has managed to recover over the past thirty years.

Sadly, whales have not participated in the recovery. In sixteen days constantly scanning the horizon, I did not see—save for my "dead island"—a single whale.

4

SAILING BLIND

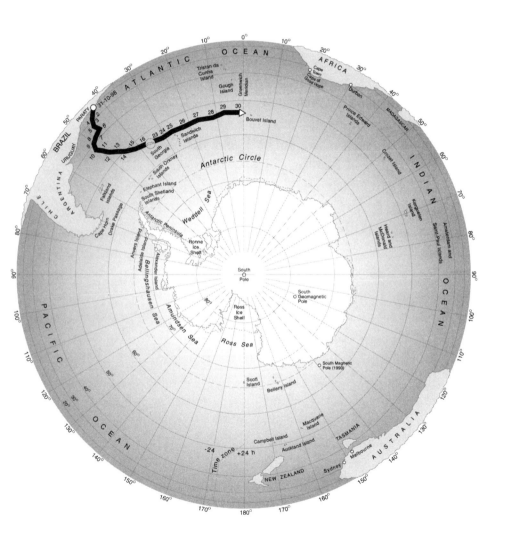

"*Wait, wait, wait, Amyr. I have something for you!*"

Hedel's intuition told her I was leaving. She and Harold had suddenly appeared on PARATII's deck. An old camera hung from Harold's neck, and Hedel was carrying an oven-fresh loaf of whole-wheat bread in a plastic bag and a small package on which were written the words: *Bon voyage, PARATII.* The package was tied with a red ribbon. By the looks of it, I figured it contained chocolate. For wrapping paper Hedel had used a page cut out of one of the dog-eared nautical almanacs. I tucked the package snugly into a corner behind the pilothouse loudspeaker, hoping the tight spot would keep it from flying loose.

The cold outside was sweet and dry, and the sunshine cast a crystal gleam on the morning. The water surrounding our boats and reaching farther to the carcasses of the DIAS and ALBATROSS, whalers of old, was spanned by a thin sheet of ice spider-cracked into random geometric figures every time the lines moved.

The 7,628-feet peak of Mount Sugar Top—Tim Carr's personal weather indicator—was clear, suggesting good weather, westerly winds, and a good time to depart. Calmly, I readied the sails before gathering in the lines. The last line, which had a bowline knot at its end, got stuck in the cleat on the old pier. Hedel quickly untangled the knot, cast off the line, and in her charming German accent shouted, "We would like to see you back before winter! Be careful, Amyr!"

Though my stay in Grytviken had been short, just one week, I felt as if I were leaving my own home. Over the past few days I had grown very close to those two receding silhouettes that still stood on the dock. They felt like family. We had enjoyed some good laughs and warm discussions about the months ahead. PARATII would be sailing eastward until she worked her way back around to that same dock, this time from the west, about three months from now. Hedel and Harold were planning their own circumnavigation, not around Antarctica, but around the calendar year, wintering in their boat, encased in ice, until summer came around again. They planned to explore the island's remote bays, when possible.

Just before rounding King Edward Point and losing sight of the dilapidated whaling station's red roofs, I give one more sternward glance. I realize that this great dream I have nurtured for so many years, of circling the earth, starting from and ending up back at the same point, will end at this very spot, several hundred meters astern. Between now and the day of my return, I will be entirely focused on making it back to that old pier. I also know how disappointed I would be if I returned prematurely, having given up. This blessed dream will only come true if I keep moving forward and complete the entire journey. Only when PARATII's bow touches those old boards again will I be able to sleep in peace. From where I stand at this moment it is hard to fathom that I can travel eastward nonstop and still return to this same spot. Can it be that the Earth is truly round?

What had those circumnavigators of yesteryear hoped to find down here? As I ponder that question, I glimpse the small hillside cemetery where Shackleton is buried, my last view of Grytviken. His gravestone, circled by white crosses, is the only one facing south, the only one that is upright. All other gravestones in the cemetery are flat.

"No, this will not be my last visit to this place!" I say in a low voice. "We'll be back in March."

*   *   *

I did not say goodbye to Tim. Early that morning he had taken off on skis to make the most of the freshly fallen snow on one of his secret fields, next to Nordenskjold Glacier. Nor did I bid farewell to the glacier itself, now glistening in the sun, deep within the bay.

Then, in a split second, everything got swallowed by a fast-rolling fog. I had to be careful not to hit Right Whale Rocks, the outermost point in Cumberland Bay, where the bay opens to the sea.

This is probably for the best, I thought, as South Georgia simply vanished, peaks, glaciers, and all. The wind was blowing twenty-five knots out of the north. I took in the first reef, sat down at the navigation table and, removing my gloves with my teeth, opened up Chart 3200. I was finally under way. I was calm. No gnawing worries of any kind.

I had divided the route into stages, to keep things simple. As waypoints for each stage, I used reference points on the ocean itself, such as islands or imaginary lines (e.g., the International Date Line), or one of the meridians that divides Earth's days into twenty four one-hour time zones. The stages would serve as psychological aids, to keep me from having to face the immense amount of white space on the charts, the absurd distance ahead: 14,000 miles.

PARATII was sailing fast, though the fresh northerly winds had not yet shown their power. I resumed my half-hour sleep routine, which was much easier this time than when I had left Paraty. My work was pleasant whenever conditions were stable. Just being away from land again was quite a relief. We would reach Bouvetøya in eight or nine days. Until then, I would have nothing to worry about, but endless sea.

A sense of well-being settles on board. The heater sputters occasionally with the pitching and rolling, but manages to function properly. The mainsheet pad eye repair is holding up well. My only concern is the lack of visibility over the bow.

Though I can't see much ahead, I am sailing the largest unbroken expanse of ocean on earth. No interruptions, no continents, no ships, whose "animated" traffic (as I like to call it) clutter oceans in other parts of the world. There is a slim possibility I might see a Russian fishing vessel or a scientific ship, but those chances are very remote indeed. Our only traffic will be the "inanimate" sort, the icebergs.

They do not appear immediately, but a few indicators begin warning me that we will be meeting icebergs soon. The water temperature drops below freezing, triggering some strange phenomena on board. Despite the little heater's best efforts, the freshwater pipes freeze, cutting the fresh water flow to the galley. With a dry faucet and a frozen pump, I am forced to draw water directly from the tanks. My Italian olive oil, a gift from Dona Ana, Marina's mother, has hardened to a bright green.

During my last trip of the day to the forepeak facilities to brush my teeth and tend to other matters of a personal nature, I found that the tooth paste was frozen hard. I had no other choice but to get my pocketknife and slice the tube. "Welcome to the Southern Ocean!" I shout, as objects clank around in the sink.

Events outside are not nearly as low key as the domestic happenings below. Before completing our second day, I have already taken in two reefs in the mainsail. The wind stiffens and, with seas rolling out of the west, causing her to surf faster and faster, PARATII suddenly skids down a wave and takes a blow on her side. This doesn't make sense, nor does it make me very happy. I decide, as a precaution, to shift rudder control from the windvane autopilot to the electronic autohelm. Perhaps the Swedish steering system failed, allowing the boat to turn, exposing her side to the waves. But, strangely, the sails have not been disturbed at all, and PARATII resumes her course.

As I make my way out to the stern platform to disconnect the windvane autopilot, I figure out what has happened: the waves are no longer acting normally. The seas are crossed, with waves coming from two directions. Every now and then a small, irreverent wave from the north slams the side of the boat without warning, giving the false impression that PARATII has lost her heading or broaches.

The barograph, which records barometric pressure on sheets in week-long intervals, first went downward for almost 20 millibars, and now shows a sharp climb. It doesn't take me long to realize that the worst weather comes not when the pressure drops steeply, but when it is climbing back to normal.

I spend most of my days at the navigation table, but often I go up on deck, hoping to see the horizon somewhere. For three days there has been no sign of it. In every direction, sky and sea merge into a uniform gray, giving me no reliable idea of what lays ahead.

By the third day the nearest land, Zavodowsky Island, lays somewhere astern. But even if the entire archipelago of the Sandwich Islands—my next landmark along the way—had been planted on the end of my nose, I don't think I would be able to see it.

Watching the pointer on my GPS, which indicates our position and heading, and counting the miles still to go—less than 1,000 to the remote little isle of Bouvetøya—I imagine the agony of earlier sailors (even fairly recent ones), who had to rely on decent visibility and celestial navigation to reach their destinations. And just to think that a mere nine years ago, this same PARATII had sailed to latitude 68° South under the guidance of nothing but a sextant and elusive stars. Blessed gadget, this GPS.

At 3:23 a.m. local time on the fourth day out, my suspicions of yesterday evening are confirmed. Slightly to starboard, one point off the bow . . . an immense tabular iceberg. I pass it with a mile to spare, deep in my thoughts. There it is, my most dangerous enemy, setting out on a journey of its own, a frozen leviathan topped by a beautiful plateau, its edges lined with jagged inlets and grottoes deep enough to swallow a boat of any size.

I am not cold. The sea has grown calmer and rather unremarkable. It could easily be just another foggy day back in Paraty or Santos. The only difference is this imposing edifice, majestic and white, alongside. It seems to have a life all its own. Water in varying shades of blue gush from its eroded sides. Its grottoes issue a thundering boom each time a wave crashes against them only to be pulverized into a vast explosion of spray. As we gain some distance, the interval grows between the waves crashing and the rumble that follows. A floating show of sounds and shapes, now falling away astern.

In a sense, this a personal welcome sent out by the Southern Ocean. I certainly get the message. This is the end of peace! The irritating ditties I tend to sing, repeated to exhaustion, suddenly stop.

Keeping one eye on the radar as we rapidly draw away from the iceberg, I decide on a lightning assault on the galley. Without losing sight of our nemesis, I manage to throw together a spaghetti *al funghi*, served up at the navigation table in front of the radar screen.

Before I finish eating, another dot appears on the little screen. Then, another. The party starts earlier than I thought. At 3:30 a.m., still doing eight to ten knots, I notice a flat iceberg between the waves. It is small, the size of a volleyball court—but this one has not appeared on the radar screen.

I miss the days when my only concerns were the weather and the seas. I decided to shorten my periods of sleep, down to fifteen minutes, until the situation improves—if it does.

*   *   *

Friday, November 27. The wind, blowing steadily between 30 and 35 knots, turns southwesterly. I would love to slow down, but I also want to get out of this situation as quickly as I can. The mainsail is reduced as much as possible, with its two reefs taken in. The number of icebergs has increased dramatically. Every type imaginable—castles, towers, fortresses, even giant bugs. At times a large tabular berg appears with its flat top stretching for hundreds of feet.

9:53 a.m. BOOM! We hit a small, eroded block of ice and then, CRUNCH! We run over another, this one even more rotten than the first, which breaks into bits. My goodness! What if it had not broken up? What if the aluminum hull had not withstood the impact? I thank God that I have a strong hull made of high-quality, thick aluminum that has, on other occasions, struck even harder rocks. But who knows how long I can go on making rudder corrections without taking my eyes off the bow? I feel a premature weariness, and I know that during my few minutes of sleep, with the boat sailing blindly along, dodging icebergs is the equivalent of playing the lottery.

Raspy, noisy, unpleasant collisions take place, but they do not cause objects inside the boat to fly around as they had earlier. As a precaution, I raise the submerged portion of the windvane autopilot, as this is the part most vulnerable to the small chunks of ice that keep passing by.

Traffic gets heavier. In the beginning I choose to pass the larger icebergs on their leeward side, though it would have been wiser to have passed them on their windward side, where the wind cleared away any ice debris. As I round these high-walled castles—sometimes coming in way too close—I hear the deafening percussion of waves exploding, even before I turn my head to look at them.

What a strange sound, so far from land, the collision of waves against solid walls of ice. After a while, I stop fleeing new bergs that pop up, and instead I begin to negotiate our distance from them, actually nudging up to some of them, dodging small bits of trailing wind-strewn ice.

Binoculars, alarm clock, radar, alarms, even a cow bell—every available implement is mustered into action. Visibility is not as bad as I had thought; the only thing that annoys me is the absence of a defined horizon and the challenge of estimating my distance from icebergs. Though the wind is strong, the sea has turned smooth.

Suddenly, a mysterious surprise. In the middle of so many frozen obstacles, the water in the pipes thaws. Pumps, faucets, olive oil, toothpaste—everything starts working again. The alarm clock is set to allow for a maximum of 20 minutes of sleep.

Those days of heavy traffic, with their bureaucratic and disciplined vigilance, are slow and tense, and feel like months of sailing. The smart thing would be to drop down to lower latitudes (to our north) to freer waters, but I am only two hundred miles from Bouvetøya, and don't want to miss the chance to see an island: a real island, one that appears on the chart, as opposed to those irksome moving islands that are constantly crossing my path.

Monday, November 30. A strange day. Since leaving Grytviken one week ago, our daily average performance has been at levels I hope to maintain over the next ten to twelve weeks. Twelve hundred miles made good, at an average of 7.3 knots. If my nerves were not so frazzled by endless detours around icebergs, I would have had good reason to celebrate.

We cross the Greenwich meridian, into the eastern hemisphere. PARATII's controversial mast is still performing flawlessly as she cruises ahead, obedient and secure.

In the early hours of the morning, however, an incident destroys all hope for future tranquility. I spend the rest of the day wondering how I have escaped utter destruction.

Before lying down for yesterday's last nap at nearly midnight, when it was already dark, I transferred control of the boat from the electronic autohelm to the windvane autopilot. I wanted to give the electric system and the batteries a rest. This kind of short nap in a dim light, at the very moment when you most need the real thing, a deep sleep through the dark of night, is the worst. For some unknown reason, I overslept. Perhaps I was more exhausted than usual; perhaps the alarm clock did not ring. Or perhaps I simply forgot to set it—I will never know.

When I open my eyes, surprise! Broad daylight. My goodness! The clock! The heading! The bow! The icebergs! It is almost 3:00 a.m. I jump from the bunk straight to the pilothouse helm, startled and frightened. I've slept like an angel for two or three periods in a row, maybe as long as two hours, without waking.

The bow! I look ahead. Thank God, no icebergs. But, when I open the companionway hatch and look aft—I freeze. Directly astern, sitting right across PARATII's wake, is an iceberg almost 1,300 feet wide. It is as if, while I slept, she sailed right over it. Or through it. It looks as if we have somehow emerged from the belly of the berg.

I am not dreaming. Right there behind me, a high-rise of ice, four city blocks long, half a city block tall, less than one mile away from PARATII. The radar confirms my sighting. The spot on the radar lays precisely in line with the route we have just traveled.

This doesn't make any sense at all. Barring some miracle that diverted PARATII, I should have at least scraped the monster's vertical walls. One of the iceberg's sides is higher than the other and leaning outward, rising at least 130 feet above the waves. I never experienced such a dreadful surprise—spared by pure chance.

At this point, there is nothing else I can do. I made an error and it is staring me in the face. I feel tremendous guilt. How did I slip by unscathed? Why didn't I wake up? I could have easily woken to find myself buried under a wall of ice, the waves grinding PARATII to pulp.

The GPS shows PARATII still making eight or nine knots, and as much as twelve or thirteen when we surf a wave. I would have preferred a thousand times over to have awaken to find that great wall ahead of me, to have fought desperately to get out of its way in the nick of time. But to accept that sheer luck saved me, this is not easy. I check the alarm clock and the red timer. Both should have sounded. I have tested them and they are working. The radar alarm, which sounds when suspicious blotches appear on the screen, is off. When we started to run into so many icebergs, and each triggered the alarm, I finally turned the blasted thing off. It doesn't matter. I have never relied on the radar alarm alone. I always shorten my naps to give me plenty of time to maneuver around obstacles.

I will never know what happened—whether PARATII maneuvered herself, or whether "someone" helped me out. Neither will I know how close we truly came to the jagged walls of that nightmare.

I go up on deck and because of the rolling deck, dangling my arms, I walk like a monkey. When I reach the bow pulpit I turn and look aft, holding onto the lifelines. I scan PARATII's full length from the point that would have struck first. I apologize to my beloved boat.

When I return below, half an hour later with my fingers hurting from the cold, the iceberg is no longer visible to the naked eye, though it still appears on the radar screen— a shiny dot that has changed my journey. Never, ever again, under any circumstances, will I be careless in properly dividing my periods of sleep and work.

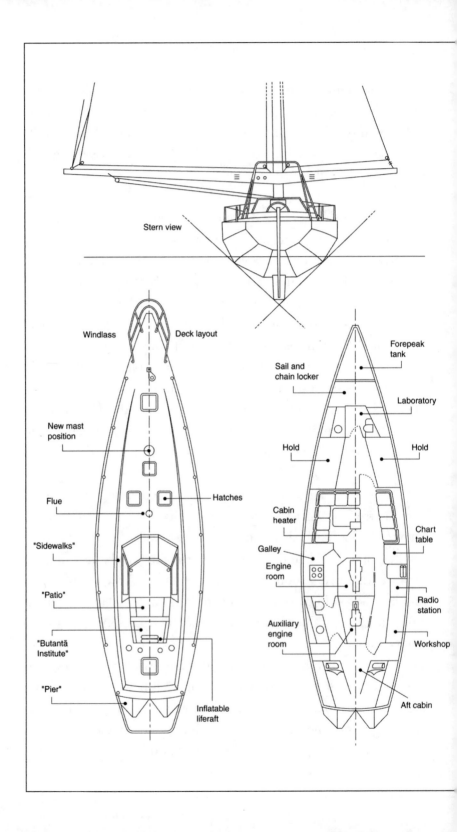

Stern view

Deck layout

Windlass

New mast
position

Flue

"Sidewalks"

"Patio"

"Butantã
Institute"

"Pier"

Hatches

Inflatable
liferaft

Sail and
chain locker

Forepeak
tank

Laboratory

Hold

Hold

Cabin
heater

Galley

Engine
room

Auxiliary
engine
room

Chart
table

Radio
station

Workshop

Aft cabin

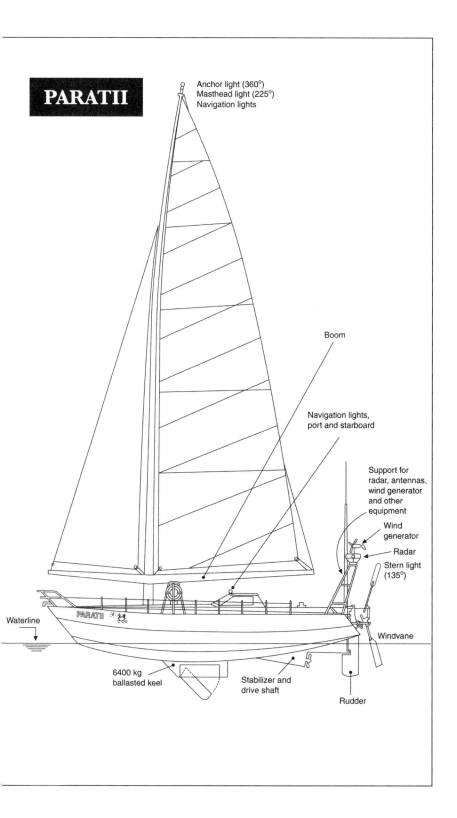

PARATII

Anchor light (360°)
Masthead light (225°)
Navigation lights

Boom

Navigation lights,
port and starboard

Support for
radar, antennas,
wind generator
and other
equipment

Wind
generator

Radar

Stern light
(135°)

Waterline

Windvane

6400 kg
ballasted keel

Stabilizer and
drive shaft

Rudder

I change the batteries in the alarm clock. Using some Velcro strips, I reposition the baking timer and the alarm clock to a distance greater than arm's length, to make sure I won't turn them off involuntarily while I am lying down. On paper, I outline the procedures for triggering the radar alarm. I extend the alarm scope on the radar screen, then test it with every new iceberg that comes into view. Still, I cannot shake free of my guilt.

Again, I go out on deck. The windvane autopilot has the helm. Suddenly, I understand. I think I am grasping at the only possible explanation, feeble as it is, for still being alive, for not having drowned in the Southern Ocean. I am staring at it.

The windvane autopilot, an admirable and sensitive mechanism, holds a sailboat on course by remaining at a constant relative angle to the wind, rather than holding it to a compass heading as an electronic autohelm would. Therefore, any small variation in wind direction causes the windvane to turn as it seeks to hold its relative angle to the wind. Every time the windvane turns, the rudder turns with it, altering the boat's heading.

This simple mechanical marvel has made it possible for tens of thousands of shorthanded and singlehanded sailors to cruise the seas, make ocean crossings, and circumnavigate the globe. Before the invention of the windvane autopilot, only a scant few extraordinary and highly-skilled sailors such as Joshua Slocum or Argentina's Vito Dumas managed to circle the earth without crew, and they did so by making constant and crafty helm adjustments. That was back when boats allowed it.

Today's boats, which are much faster and more spirited, rarely allow such adjustments. Often, modern boats do not adapt to even the simplest of windvane autopilot systems and require powerful electronic systems in order to free the sailor from the slavish task of sitting at the helm for days on end.

PARATII is an unusually happy boat in this respect, thanks in part to the way my friend, Cabinho, designed her, giving her a balanced and seaworthy hull. Also Furia, the engineer, and I had placed high priority on her rudder design, in the knowledge that she would often be sailed short- or single-handed. I do not like to touch the helm once I am at sea, and somehow we had gotten things right on PARATII. I was certain about this when I decided to undertake the voyage. Furthermore, the new mast had added enormously to PARATII's responsiveness and stability, despite the disastrous predictions of skeptics.

Not for anything in the world, money or trophies, would I undertake the insane endeavor of sailing down here alone without an efficient steering system or in a boat not armed with a perfectly balanced helm. Cheap, tiny electronic steering systems, for example the Autohelm 2000, made for boats with one-fourth the displacement of PARATII, could have steered her with ease. And the windvane autopilot, in winds from six to 60 knots, never failed to function with precision. This balance is my boat's greatest quality, a quality absent in most sailboat designs I know.

Therefore, the only explanation for our having "bypassed" the iceberg is the windvane autopilot. Given the average height of a tabular iceberg, which is 130 to 160 feet— twice the height of my mast and maybe four times the height of the center of wind effort with the second reef taken in— it is quite possible that, while I was sleeping, the wind that drove me toward the walls of ice deflected off the sides of the iceberg. This wind change would have triggered a correction in the windvane autopilot, causing PARATII to round the ice, keeping a constant angle relative to the wind all the way around, until the wind again straightened itself out.

Is that even possible? I don't know. But I will accept this explanation for the duration of the voyage. And I swear an oath to myself not to mention it to anyone until I return to the wooden pier at Grytviken. Whether it was God that saved us, I cannot say. I don't like to think that way. Certainly God must have far greater concerns than saving blind-sailing boats and slumbering sailors in these desolate latitudes.

5

BOUVETØYA—
THE FOGGY ISLAND

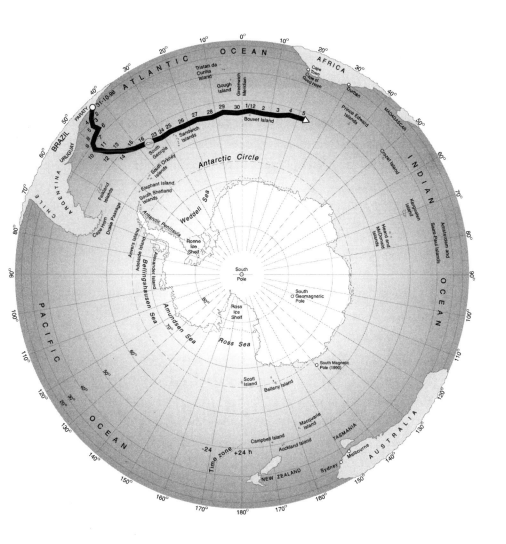

According to the British publication *Antarctic Pilot*, Bouvetøya, or Bouvet Island, is the most isolated piece of land on the planet. The island is a solitary volcanic cone 1,020 nautical miles southeast of Gough Island and 1,370 miles southwest of the Cape of Good Hope. It was discovered almost miraculously by French Commandant Bouvet de Lozier during the summer of 1739. Bouvet had shipped out the year before from Brazil's Santa Catarina Island. Like so many sailors of that era, he hoped to discover a continent or other unknown lands around the South Pole. His ships, the MARIE and the AIGLE, sailed through seventy days of nonstop foul-weather and fog. When they reached latitude 48°S, the two ships began a forty-day sojourn among icebergs, slogging through snow flurries, sleet, and zero visibility. Though they struggled to keep each other within sight, the truth was that both ships were quite lost. Bouvet's navigation logs clearly show the inaccuracies in their longitude calculations.

Amazingly, on January 1, 1739, in a rare moment of visibility, members of the expedition sighted this tiny, lonely island, the only piece of land in this vast expanse of open sea. The island was connected to an ice field, so Bouvet named his discovery Cape Circumcision, believing it to be the Antarctic continent. For twelve days the ships tried to approach or circle the land, but the ice stopped them on every attempt. On January 12, with their crews weakened by exhaustion and cold, the ships turned for Cape of Good Hope, having failed to recognize that "Cape" Circumcision was not a continent after all, but a mere island—the most desolate island in the world.

In 1772, British Captain James Cook, in command of the RESOLUTION, undertook the mission of investigating the Frenchman's discovery. Following Bouvet's error-ridden logs, he made several fruitless attempts to locate Bouvet, ultimately hoping to find the continent itself.

In 1774, RESOLUTION's sister ship, ADVENTURE, commanded by Tobias Furneaux, and the next year Cook's RESOLUTION tried yet again, but with no success. In 1843, British Captain James Ross and his legendary ships, EREBUS and TERROR, repeated the effort, but this too failed. Confirmation that Bouvet was only an island did not come until 1908, when the whalers SNOW SWAN and OTTER, belonging to the Enderby brothers and commanded by James Lindsay and Thomas Hopper, sailed around it. Their inability to break through the ice fields kept them three miles away from the island itself.

In 1922, the American sealer, WASP, under the command of Captain Benjamin Morrell, was the first ship to actually land on the island. In December 1929, a Norwegian expedition claimed possession of the island, christening it Bouvetøya, Norwegian for Bouvet Island, in honor of the French explorer.

Tuesday, December 1. At noon local time the GPS shows 54°12.50' S and 02°42.73'E. The island is only 25 miles away, but I can't see farther than the length of a football field. The fog is fluffy, cottonlike. The radar screen shows three large icebergs off to our side, many more up ahead, but not one of them is visible to the naked eye. This will be my last opportunity to see the island.

I swing PARATII's bow around to the north. Five minutes later, Bouvetøya is on the radar—23.7 miles ahead. I come onto the northern side of the island bank. The depth reading, which was in kilometers, suddenly registers mere meters. I can almost smell the nearby land. The wind is straight out of the north at 25 knots, shrieking in my ears. I go up to the bow once again. No sign of the island. I am surrounded by fog, fog, and more fog—and did I mention the icebergs?

When I walk by the mast, I loosen the mainsail halyard and take in a second reef. I also shorten the jib. We need to move slowly, I think. I run back to the cockpit to find some dry gloves. My fingers are freezing from handling wet lines. Six miles to go . . . five . . . approaching. I am standing out on the bow pulpit, and I see nothing. The radar is set to a one-mile scale with six-mile scope. The blotch on the screen keeps growing. Three miles out, I can't take it anymore. "Where are you, Bouvetøya? Where?" Ice is everywhere around us now. Small chunks emerge from the cottony fog ahead. Other than that, I can't see or hear anything but the wind.

"Tear my hull in this godforsaken place, just so I can see an island? No way! That's it! I've had it with islands around here!"

I disengage the windvane autopilot, come about, sheet the boom home, and head back into the wind.

"Away from the island, immediately!" I shout my orders to the crew of one.

I remove my left-hand glove and with my fingers still frozen hard I write in my log: *Farewell, Bouvetøya, foggy queen I've never seen!*

11h 59min 55sec, and counting—56, 57, 58, 59, mark! I record the position. 52°58.04'S and 12°40.58'E! This is the high point of each day to record my position at 1200 GMT. It is recorded in the log, to serve as a reference point for gauging my performance over the previous twenty-four hours. I rely on these daily records to estimate the distance remaining at each stage.

Our latest progress, 192 miles, traveled over the past 24 hours, brings our daily average to 172! We had reached the +1 time

Breaking through the ice fields

zone (GMT time "plus one hour") a little ahead of my projections. If we can maintain the average we managed over the last ten days, covering five degrees of longitude per day, we should be entering a new time zone every three days. Isn't it funny how good moods are so often the product not of what we actually see outside, but of what we perceive internally when we accomplish simple objectives? Watching PARATII hit her performance objectives does wonders for the general mood on board.

Our steady progress eastward throws off our schedules and daily appointments. Sailing with the rotation of the earth, eastward, and absorbing a full hour every three days (or every 15 degrees), means that each day is twenty minutes shorter than its predecessor. One degree of eastward sailing shaves four minutes off each day. At the rate we are traveling, my days are shorter than those of anyone standing still, anywhere on earth. As a result, pre-scheduled appointments—such as radio contacts with Brazil, which are always set for 8:00 p.m. local time (or 2200 GMT)—keep coming later and later into our "local day." Days grow shorter for those who sail eastward, longer for those who sail westward. It's that simple. But to record the fact—twenty minutes knocked off every day—is one of the small pleasures I enjoy while plotting our daily position on the big chart.

Another peculiarity of long voyages in high latitudes has to do with total distance covered. The farther south I go, the shorter the distance I need to travel. In the lower latitudes, near the tropics, changes in distances are so slight as to be almost imperceptible. But not here. On the equator, one degree of longitude is the same in length as one degree of latitude—sixty nautical miles. Along my home latitude, in Paraty, around 23°30'S, one must travel 55 miles, either east or west, to traverse one degree of longitude. Further south, at 50°S, we only have to travel 38.6 nautical miles to span the distance from one degree to another. And when we reach 60°S—my target latitude, to be reached around the mid-way point across the Pacific Ocean—we will be ticking off one degree of latitude for every thirty nautical miles made good.

I rework the distance figures (in degrees of latitude), both for minutes of distance made good, and for days sailing. I then re-draw the stages I had penciled earlier onto General Chart No. 4009, the most beautiful chart of all—the master chart I used for planning the entire voyage. If everything goes according to my carefully laid plans, one day this chart will show the position markings for the entire journey, a line connecting dots all the way around Antarctica. I have not yet used this chart on the voyage. The distances are overwhelming and daily progress is so minus-cule, even discouraging.

Printed in imposing letters across the chart, are the words *Terra Australis Nondum Cognita*; (unknown south land), Antarctica. Wrapping its way 360 degrees around the continent is the ocean I am now traveling. It has no name in Portuguese, and in English it is called simply the Southern Ocean. Radiating upward and outward from it, like spokes or wedges, are the Atlantic, Indian, and Pacific Oceans, the boundaries of which are formed by the southern extremities of South America, Africa, and Tasmania.

Inspired by yesterday's good performance and by the fact that I dodged the heavy iceberg traffic, I take out the large nautical chart from the drawer under the navigation table. It is still folded in the conventional fashion and wrapped in an enormous plastic envelope (a precaution against any wet surprises). Because my table is so small I have to fold the chart into twelve squares, a sac-rilege to those conventional mariners who have access to large navigation tables and lots of space. I don't have that kind of space on PARATII, so I am limited to working with one face of the folded chart at a time, in stages.

I begin plotting our daily noon GMT position on the General Chart, drawing tiny triangles. Beside each triangle I write the date, the number of days out, and the distance made good. The first four triangles of the voyage are missing because their spaces were off the edge of the chart. Those marks have been plotted on a Mercator chart of Brazil.

Since leaving South Georgia I have accumulated ten triangles—1,800 miles made good, 53 degrees of eastward progress—almost fifteen percent of the 360 degrees are staring back at me from the chart.

I spend the day buried in the chart, working furiously. I have a duplicate of No. 4009, so I decide to plot our positions on both charts. This is a rather pointless redundancy, but a pleasant exercise because it allows me to see the immensity of our route.

By the time I finish the chart-plotting tasks, night has fallen. The hours flew by unnoticed. I can't remember how many sleep periods I have missed. I feel good, am in great physical shape (about 18 pounds lighter), and my sleep patterns are comfortably under control.

In the evening, at the scheduled time for radio contact with Brazil, propagation fails. I have begun to count on the invisible friendly presence of our chat group on the fifteen-meter bandwidth, 14 255 MHZ. Five or six of us are regular ham radio operators, in addition to América, PY5AEV and Ulysses, PY2UAJ. Ulysses, who is having antenna problems, coordinates the contacts, sometimes without even coming onto the frequency himself. Then there is América, my ham "angel." She is an expert at finding propagation windows to link families with loved ones on distant boats. She always comes on with a loud, bright signal from her home in Curitiba. Laslo, PY2LG (a.k.a. "Lima Golf"), will "go fishing" until he picks me up on the frequency; he has the most experience in the group. I had never met him personally, but he became a father figure in our chats. The other regular members of that fifteen-meter family include Lopes (PY2SM), Nerley (PY2NP), Guido (PY2GIG), and Bueno (PY2BVY). Sometimes there are other call signs and voices that slowly become friends. The world of amateur radio is imbued with a spirit of solidarity and support that simply does not exist in any other form of communications, including the Internet. Internet and cellular communications will certainly affect radio traffic around the world. But their effect will not be felt as quickly at sea as on land. For one thing, electromagnetic waves cost nothing and, with patience and skill, the greatest feats of human-to-human contact are possible.

It is a great relief to leave Bouvetøya behind. It is a pity not to have spotted the island, even though I came within three miles of its shores. Yet another island will now be added to my wish-list for future visits. The parade of ships and expeditions that made their way down here only to fail to see or set foot on the island is spectacular. Nevertheless, it feels good to know that the island is behind me now and that we are free from the nerve-wracking mix of fog, ice, and wind. I am relieved and this seems to me to be more valuable right now than sighting Bouvetøya, a rather useless geographic achievement.

I am unhappy sometimes thinking about how many miles still lay ahead, or how much time remains until the end of the voyage. But what bothers me even more is that the heater started acting up. I know I can't keep it on much longer.

After a heavy squall passes through, PARATII will often pitch and roll so violently that both boom ends take turns dipping into the crests of the waves. This motion upset the heater. At first I thought wind gusts were working their way into the chimney and causing the heater to sputter. I covered the chimney with a basket woven of a vine and bamboo from Paraty, hoping it would block the gusts.

As it turns out, the problem is something else altogether. Every time PARATII rides to the top of one wave and then races down before the next wave, the air pressure below decks changes dramatically. This pressure change increases the carbonization of burnt diesel, causing the heater to cough, and smoke to billow around the boat's interior.

If technical reasons alone are not enough to convince me, then at least in the interest of public health I need to start thinking about turning off the heater. As it is, the benefits of heat below decks, in the galley and the saloon, are minimal at best. It is cold any way you look at it. But, from down there, the heat rises . . . up to the pilothouse where I spend most of my time, providing a measure of warmth to the area around the navigation table and my bunk, as well as holding humidity to decent levels.

Back to the remaining miles and the long months ahead: I know the comforts I enjoyed thus far will not remain with me for the entire journey. The weather, though challenging with zero visibility, lots of ice and strong winds, has not dealt any violent blows. We have not yet run into monumental waves, infernal winds—these famous natural forces in these latitudes—but they are sure to come. When they will threaten PARATII with a knockdown or capsize, I don't want to have diesel burning down below. But I am fond of my little bonfire (that's what I call the heater), and as long as conditions will allow, the little bonfire will keep burning.

The whole Bouvetøya episode was important, or, more precisely, it was a period of indoctrination on watch procedures. Never again will I be caught off-guard again by a stupid sleep-related error, only to be crucified against a wall of ice.

Thoughts of crucifixion remind me of a doomsayer friend's words. Though he is a good sailor, he didn't like my new mast. He pestered me about it, to the point of getting me mad.

"Bah! What a horrible thing this is!" he would say. "It's nothing but a white cross; you're going to drive it into the ground!"

"I'm going to drive it into your miserable head when I get home," I thought. Needless to say, by "drive it into the ground" he actually meant "capsize."

I keep myself busy every day, focused on not making any mistakes, not "driving crosses into the ground," and hitting our longitude goals on time, all of which brings a welcome benefit: it makes time pass. I have begun to divide the days into segments. I manage each segment by monitoring its contribution to our daily and weekly performance averages. I am starting to live in the present, not thinking about next month, taking advantage of every smooth-sailing minute to catch up on sleep, and of every second of calm to work my way down my to-do list.

Sometimes I have to make repairs, though not too many. Most are preventive: invert the autopilot lines, grease the rudder shaft and bearings, change out a chafed line over here, check for wear over there, adjust the position of the reefing lines, and so forth. But any time the seas become heavy the tasks start to pile atop one another.

For the first time I miss having books to read. I brought along 200 pounds of good books: some original expedition accounts, sailing classics, and poetry in French. One was a spectacular book about the history of Siberia, brilliantly written but not easy reading. Anything I read that mentions ice, cold, boats or rhymes puts me right to sleep. I miss cheap books, detective stories, throwaway romances, anything that doesn't carry the smell of the sea. I miss books that could have made time pass, that could have taken my thoughts far away.

ENDLESS SEA

* * *

The coordinates that marked the end of this stage are 51°30'S, 72°00'E—south of the Kerguelen Islands, 2,000 miles ahead of our current position. If the density of iceberg traffic increases, I will head a bit to the north, but no further than 51°S. If PARATII maintains her current averages, I am on track to reach my waypoint in thirteen days, when we will cross the meridian that runs through the islands.

In the early hours of Thursday morning, my tenth day out of South Georgia, the skies opened up for the first time. Somehow an incandescent moon exploded over the oily seas, though it only lasted two hours. The stars were out; the night was smooth and quiet. How about that!

At the first hint of daybreak, fog rolled in again. No sun in sight. In fact, I hadn't seen the sun in 2,000 miles and still had no idea where the horizon line was. All I could see was that constant undefined area where sky and sea blend into each other. With each successive day of fog and snow my thoughts returned to those men who had come here long before, to discover land where only ice could be seen, navigating by heavenly bodies that never made an appearance, and relying on an uncertain horizon.

Every time I entered or exited through the narrow companionway, I squeezed the wooden handrail with my fingers. Any time I was not wearing gloves, I tapped the wood three times—a gesture that became automatic over time, my sincerest expression of gratitude to PARATII for the simple fact that she had carried me this far while sparing me any serious breakdowns.

I sail into Sunday, December 6, as if I were sailing into the glassy bay of Jurumirim. Flat calm, again. It is hard to imagine, sitting on this oily sea, that this is the same Indian Ocean that begins at Cape of Good Hope, 1,050 miles north of here. Not the slightest wave. Sails slap this way and that, lost, unsupported. The only irritating sound in this entire region is the jib traveler slamming back and forth.

At 2:30 a.m., already daylight, visibility improves. I am about to celebrate my second ice-free day when, uh-oh! a spot on the radar. I go up on deck and, sure enough, an enormous iceberg. It is recorded in the log as, *Our first Indian Ocean berg!*

I travel through the night with the engine running to charge the batteries. It pushes us along at about seven knots. Just before 4:00 a.m., a puff of wind arrives out of the north. As we gather speed, I shut off the engine. I climb onto the boom to trim the mainsail when, suddenly, a huge square head rises out of the water just a few feet abeam.

"Can it be?" A sperm whale!

It is. Finally, a toothed whale! Its huge forehead pushes steadily through the water. It circles around and comes back, even closer this time. It lifts two fins from its right side almost touching the side of the boat, and then calmly swims away. I am happy to have been "almost touched" by a sperm whale, the first I ever encountered, a species I only read about in books.

Sperm whales are the rarest among the five species hunted during the South Georgia whaling era, between 1904 and 1965. In sixty-one years of heavy hunting, only 3,716 of the 175,250 whales slaughtered were sperm whales.

We are at 25°E, almost five degrees beyond the longitude of Cape Agulhas, having traveled 1,300 miles since my last whale sighting on Day Six out of South Georgia Island. I saw no mammals at all since then, until this sperm whale appeared. This is a sad fact. On South Georgia, colonies of elephant seals and other seals that had almost become extinct are back, even in bigger numbers than in the early 1900s. This is not true for whales, not after six decades of systematic slaughter. Even now, over thirty years after whale hunting was brought to a virtual halt, whale populations of the Antarctic Convergence have no guarantee of ever recovering their numbers.

In the past two weeks, images of Grytviken's whaling factory ruins have become distant. I wonder what Harold and Hedel are doing right now. Perhaps Pauline is already in New York to announce publication of her book, following so many years on the island without having seen so much as a city, or a car.

I still have a piece of the bread Hedel gave me, which I have stored in the oven. It is rock-hard, preserved by the 0° Celsius in the galley. Using a butcher's knife on a wooden cutting board, I cut four thin slices. Toasted and buttered—true delicacies each— they become part of my breakfast.

6

THE FIRST SUN

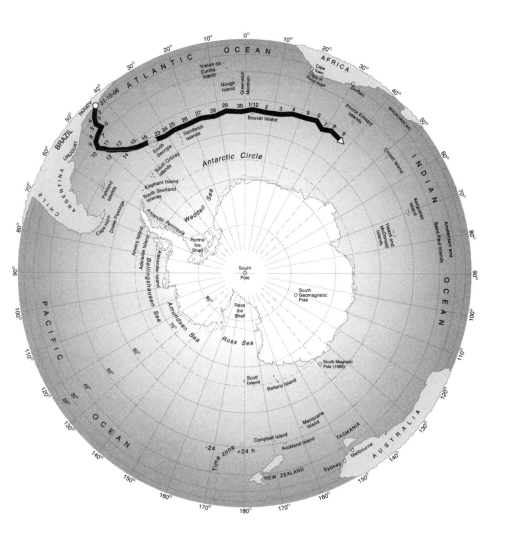

A fantastic scene spread out before us. On one side of the road, a forest higher and denser than those of the Paraty coastal range; on the opposite side, only a few trunks still upright in an ash-covered wasteland of burned trees. Most of the trees that had once stood here now lay smoldering on the ground like hot coals. The humidity was stifling, a strange product not of sunshine, but of smoke and fire. A burn forest for miles on end.

We had spent two and half days on a ferry, from Belém to Macapá, rounding the island of Marajó. Finally, we were back to making good time. At that speed, the car's suspension was reacting to the dirt roads and endless rows of deep ruts due to erosion. Hermann was driving; I was trying to sleep through the pounding ride, but I couldn't stop thinking how stupid it is to build roads instead of ports in the Amazon region. Okay, so this wasn't the Amazon region, in the strictest sense of the word. We were on the northern side of the Amazon River in the state of Amapá, headed for the Oiapoque River, toward the end of our journey, our holidays, our free time. We were near Brazil's border with Guyana, facing a 2,500-mile trip back home. We had spent the past three months crammed into two F-1000 pickups, taking in dust, dirt, asphalt, and the sea in our attempt to photograph the lighthouses—every single one of them—that line the Brazilian coast from Uruguay to the Oiapoque River. We were almost finished.

We had 250 miles to go and, if we wasted no time, we would arrive in time to see the *Círio do Nazaré*—a religious festival in honor of the patron saint of the state of Pará—making its way down the Oiapoque River. But all we could see at the moment was dust and smoke, seemingly going on forever. One forest fire followed another. In a place so inherently rich, you had to wonder what sort of economic development, what kind of wealth, could make this sort of destruction worthwhile. Why build bad roads that lead only to destruction and poverty when there is so much ocean and so many rivers along which to travel?

As I was cursing the road, the road sought its revenge. The punishment was swift. With a loud bang, the car ahead skidded to a stop. We all jumped out to see what had happened. My guess— a blown-out tire—was wrong. It was the suspension. I grabbed the jack, raised the car, and Hermann removed the wheel. The front spring had broken in half! I sat on the floor. Damn! I never dreamed of packing a spare spring. We did have two cars and a formidable arsenal of spare parts—but a spring? Our two other partners, Lobão and André, were experienced Paris-Dakar Rally racers, but not even they knew how to fix this problem.

I went over and dug up the junk box. It was full of scraps left over from when I had built PARATII. At the start of the lighthouse trip, the guys had teased me mercilessly about this box.

As it stood now, we were facing at least a week-long delay if we tried to find a phone or drive back to Macapá to find a replacement part.

I threw the box in the bed of the truck, spread the zillions of scraps out so I could see them, and took a seat on the ground. As I perused that pile of junk, an idea sprang to life. I found a string of steel rings the Suprens Company had given me many years ago. With my bare hands, I twisted the spring in a counter-spiral direction, about a two-thirds turn. Using the rings and wooden wedges cut from dead trees, I fashioned a very primitive repair. Hermann poured water on the wooden wedges to make them swell and fill the spaces. The spring had surrendered less than a full turn of its spiral; the difference was hardly noticeable. Most surprising was the fact that the repair not only worked but withstood 750 miles of potholes before we got to a dealership.

The truth is that the junk box saved me countless times. There was no apparent logic to its contents, just leftovers from prior voyages or building projects. Bits of this and that: cotter pins, parts, scrap, and junk—nothing was rejected as long as it fit in the box. When problems arose and no solutions were forthcoming, I always turned to it. To explore the box's contents was to engage in an exercise in creativity. If I ever failed to find the little part needed to solve my immediate problem, at least I now knew what was missing, or what I had forgotten. Ventures into the junk box invariably ended either in exuberant celebrations or kick-the-can tantrums.

PARATII generated three types of scrap: general purpose, electrical, and hydraulic. Three piles of junk, kept in reasonable order, in three distinct boxes. We had made a giant leap forward, thanks to my friends Giacomo and Luiz, who spent over a month coding each item on board, including each little scrap in those boxes, and entering them into a database.

I am concerned that the lines that engage the windvane autopilot wear out unevenly, until a deck inspection reveals that the red line and the windvane arm are impregnated with a lead-colored dust. Though the self-steering system is working flawlessly, something isn't right. The dust indicates friction somewhere, aluminum on aluminum, and that doesn't look good. Perhaps there is friction on the drive shaft or one of the ball-bearing blocks. Problems . . . hmmm.

I go after the old scrap box, stowed in the starboard salon locker. I raise the cushion, unlatch the lid to the locker, pull out the box, and within minutes fish out all the materials I need to attempt a repair. I even find some Delrin bearings and single sheaves that my friend Amilcar, from the Nautec Company, sent me decades ago. Thank God they haven't slithered into some unreachable corner somewhere.

The problem has to do with regulating the control arms. For over 40,000 miles before embarking on this voyage, PARATII always used a windvane autopilot just like this one. For years it had performed the solitary work of holding my boat's heading, and there had never been a problem. The manufacturer, Sailomat, had suggested that I exchange the old system for a new and, allegedly, vastly improved model.

I fell for the pitch presented by Mr. Knoos, Sailomat's Swedish president and inventor of the windvane autopilot. A one-week engineering course is all that would have been required to notice, after testing the product, that the device's geometry of effort had been shifted—we could call it an improvement in the wrong direction. Anytime engineering solutions stray from practical experience, there is a high likelihood of committing this very sort of error. The fact that we are 8,000 miles from home, traveling a less-than-forgiving route, gives the error an exponential magnitude.

From the moment I first installed the new system at Pier 26, I had my doubts about the boasts behind Mr. Knoos's modifications, so I decided not to get rid of the old system just yet, but rather to stow it in a box in the stern locker. This annoyed me, because it seemed wasteful to carry poorly designed equipment (and it was a heavy item) on board—equipment that would be responsible for a significant amount of PARATII's steering and my general safety. Though I am still grateful to the contraption for having steered me clear of that iceberg, I won't be able to sleep well until I repair it or at least figure out what is wrong with it. The old model had never had this problem.

Because I do not care to dangle off the stern, hanging out over the water, running the risk of watching cotter pins, tiny nuts, washers, and other of Mr. Knoos's technological absurdities sink 4,000 meters to the ocean floor, I choose instead to dismantle the entire device and haul it inside where, in the comfort of PARATII's workshop, I will be able to work without my fingers frozen stiff. Though this idea includes more challenges and is infinitely more labor-intensive, it is also less risky. I spend an entire hour out on deck laying out step-by-step plans for executing the operation. PARATII's rolling deck, her speed, the absence of handholds, and even the risk of a rogue wave remove all doubt: the attempt to drag this huge piece of hardware across the deck is sure to be a high-drama circus act. Though I am accustomed to running along the deck like a quadruped, using hands and feet, a simian's prehensile tail would come in handy right now, the better to hang on to wrenches and other tools.

Five hours later, a biped again, grasping the stern arch, I celebrate the end of the operation. I gather my wits about me again, I recheck the entire system, and by nightfall the torrent of oaths cast in the general direction of the Swedish engineer has subsided.

I guess Mr. Knoos called forth a plague while I was re-installing his windvane autopilot, because when I return below, PARATII's interior has become a walk-in freezer. The heater stopped working. My cozy boat is now a meat locker.

This means yet another hour of hard work—indoors, this time—cleaning ducts and carbon buildup. It is colder below than outside—a psychological cold in a smoke-filled environment that reminds me of those Amapá forest fires. After several failed attempts I am forced to surrender. I do what Hermann would have done: chanting in jest, I go out on deck and shout to whoever might be listening, "Goodbye! Goodbye comfort! Now it's time to freeze our ass!"

The First Sun

That is the coldest night of the entire voyage. To top it all, the wind has clocked ninety degrees to the east, on the nose. This means that just before every sleep period I have to tack, crafting a zigzag pattern upwind, and dropping our daily distance average to its lowest level of the entire voyage.

This is a national embarrassment, or rather, an international one: twenty-four hours of tacking produced a miserable 84 miles made good. And the good times aren't over yet. Wind on the nose is bad enough, but this wind is erratic. The seas are heavy. Every time the wind dies, the sails go slack, robbing the boom of its much-needed support and causing it to swing wildly back and forth. As I rig a preventer to subdue it, a lovely ice-cold rain bursts upon us. This is the real thing, this rain; not sleet or snow, but Amazonian-style torrential rain.

Despite all setbacks—the nasty weather, the pathetic rate of progress, and the damp cold that will be my close companion from now on—the mood on board is undergoing a subtle shift. However poor our progress might be at the moment, to turn back would be even worse.

Though we have dropped below my projected daily average, I expect soon to find opportunities to recover lost ground. PARATII is shipshape. If the Swedish windvane autopilot fails again, I will send it down the Prince Edward fracture—that's 2,500 meters straight down—and I will install the old system in its place. Or I will turn to the electronic autopilots. I have solutions for those sorts of problems. Things could be much worse: I could be sick, unprepared or injured.

About the heater: if we were to capsize, I know the heater would be a hazard. It is best to save the heater and fuel. They will come in handy when I pull into Dorian Bay.

I have plenty of cold-weather gear, and it is time to start

wearing it properly. I am thinking of the racing sailors, whose lives are infinitely more difficult. They use only one foul-weather jacket for an entire voyage, racing blindly through the Atlantic Convergence's minefields in plastic hulls so thin they are virtually transparent. Of course, I am a huge admirer of those men and women who take on that challenge—especially those who do it singlehanded. But to compete for a trophy, a medal, or money . . . way down here? That seems completely idiotic.

Not to be free to choose your route, or to act of your own free will, under the risk of a penalty or of being disqualified, without being able to make any stopovers at all? I am thinking about that as I lay in my cozy bunk with my boots and gloves on, arms behind my head, comfortable in dry clothes. If these get wet, I'll just change them for dry clothes stowed down below. I am my own boss, accountable only to myself, following my nose.

Talking about nose, I am just now pointing it toward the bow. I see a distinct cloud of fog. I turn my head to the side, toward the radar—nothing. I jump out of bed. Damm! It is a little orphan iceberg. Damn! Damn! We're going to hit it! I run to disengage the self-steering mechanism, take over the helm, make a slight swerve, reengage the self-steering, and crawl back into bed. By a hair . . .

Thirty minutes later, at 52°13'S and 27°58'E, the mother of the baby iceberg appears, an immense tabular sheet moving north, one and a half miles away, so close I feel I could reach out and touch her.

"Let's just look; don't touch," I say softly.

As bad as it feels to be so cold, rising and falling over the waves of the Indian Ocean, it would have been worse not to have gotten this far, or never to have left the warm and comfortable waters of Paraty, even if only to better appreciate how warm and comfortable those waters are. I feel an unusual calm, dodging icebergs so far from home.

These days I understand my father very well. A man needs to travel. On his own, not through stories, images, books, or television. He needs to travel for himself, with his own eyes and on his own feet, to understand what is his. So that he might someday plant his own trees and value them. He must know cold in order to enjoy heat. And vice versa. He must experience distance and homelessness in order to feel at home under his own roof. A man needs to travel to places he does not know; he must lose the arrogance that causes him to see the world as he imagines it, rather than simply as it is, or as it can be; the arrogance that turns us into professors and doctors of what we have not seen, when we should be students who simply go and see. Jacques Cousteau, an admirable man, commenting on the success of his first major film, said, "It is no use, it will do no good; you must go see." *Il faut aller voir.* The pure truth is that the world on television may be beautiful, but it has little useful purpose. You must question what you have learned. You must go and touch it.

What is touching me now is this insidious cold that has settled on board. Actually, it has not crept in from outside, but rather from the bottom of the boat. As I try to adapt to this new and uncomfortable crewmember, I realize very quickly how pleasant sailing had been up until the present longitude.

The sadness I feel on that first day without a heater doesn't last long, barely through the first night. Nevertheless, I will never again be free of the cold until I make landfall in a sheltered bay where I will once again be able to light the heater. Night and day our new crewmember makes itself known, stalking around the boat. Steam is coming out of my nostrils.

Under my foul-weather gear I wear a new layer of polyester

clothing, the kind mountain climbers wear. And I begin to wear gloves at all times, even when I use the head. Some gloves are thin, others are heavy-duty, but none of them are truly waterproof. After I handle wet lines on deck, I send my gloves below to take their place along a drip-line where, in theory anyway, they will dry out. I have divided my glove wardrobe into quadrants, by condition: dry, wet, saltwater, and freshwater (i.e., saltwater *wet*, freshwater *dry*, and so forth).

The weekly thermograph records show a drop of almost twelve degrees in average temperatures. And, worse: the hygrograph shows that humidity below decks jumped from 60%–70% to well over 80%.

The cold has triggered some changes in the galley, too; some minor changes to the menu. I almost drowned at the navigation table when a crockpot bean soup covered the windows and portholes with steam. From now on, recipes calling for more than ten minutes of cooking time, not my favorites anyway, are dropped from the menu because they create spectacular condensation below.

Little by little, life returns to normal.

Radio propagation with Brazil, as expected, began to deteriorate until my friend América, tireless explorer of the airwaves, discovered an address and a time when I could radio home. It has been a long time. It is great to hear everyone. Hermann comes on directly from his office. Júlio is there, making preparations for his own descent to Antarctica in January as a crewmember on KOTIC, a steel sailboat belonging to a Frenchwoman named Sophie. The boat was built in Brazil and ran charter cruises between Patagonia and the Antarctic Peninsula. Our plan is to attempt a rendezvous at which he will toss me a suitcase full of news, a new version of the Iridium telephone, and photos from home, of the girls. I am overcome with emotion when I hear the twins and Marina. They have been tuned in throughout the conversation. In the background I can hear the girls' tiny unintelligible voices. Out here, surrounded by darkness, it is 1:00 a.m; in São Paulo it is 9:00 p.m.

Before signing off, América patches me into a Brazilian sailboat, ANNY, which belongs to Crespo and Raul, from the state of Paraná. Their signal is strong. They are just above me at latitude 30° in the Indian Ocean, 1,320 miles to the north. By coincidence we are sitting on the same meridian, though headed in opposite directions. ANNY is closing in on Durban, having almost completed a five-year voyage around the world. From Durban they will continue toward the Atlantic Ocean. They hope to reach Brazil by early next year, though they will make some stops along the Garden Coast on their way to Cape Town.

PARATII, on the other hand, is still heading eastward in the early stages of her circumnavigation. My plan is to be in Paraty by early next year. With any luck at all I will be reunited with the girls before their second birthday, at the end of March.

I turn off the radio, unable to take my eyes off the photo of the twins playing on the beach in Jurumirim. I imagine the smell of their hair, and their voices—my three girls. I go to sleep at 3:00 a.m., when it is already daylight.

I am homesick. It is a true physical pain; the pain that comes with missing a loved one so much; the pain of longing to touch and see. I have never felt this pain before, a mixture of pleasure, of anxiety, of unending love. There is only one remedy for this kind of pain: move on, move quickly, and remain alert.

After 17 days of absence, as if in homage to a rare star, the fog dissipates and the sun rises in the east, its rays shining through the bow porthole and beating against the back of the cockpit. Now that I think about it, it would have been sad not to feel that pain.

Before going to bed, I stand on the cockpit chair and stick my head out through the overhead hatch. With half of my body outside, facing the sun, and my hair yanked back by the wind, I shout, "Long live the sun; long live the pain I feel."

7

CHANGING LONGITUDES:
FROM THE KERGUELENS
TO CHRISTMAS ISLAND

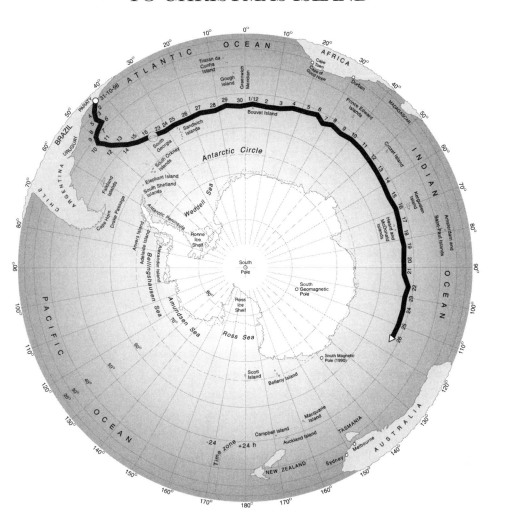

A note on the galley wall reads: "We hereby notify the crew that culinary activities will cease at 6:00 p.m. Kerguelen time—1300 UTC. Signed: The Cook."

Of course a little warmth and a ray of sunshine on calm seas help, but nothing improves more the mood around here than forging ahead. Good sailing is the overriding goal and governs all onboard decisions. Even in matters of personal comfort, painful sacrifices are willingly made to improve daily performance. To sum up, "The faster I get out of this place, the better."

Since passing south of Prince Edward and Marion Islands, the seas have changed. For the first time I can appreciate the sheer size of the Southern Ocean. Accustomed as I am to the waters of Paraty, I was intimidated at first, awed by the towering waves. Steep walls and huge trenches roll toward me from astern. My eyes are glued to their height.

Every now and then I watch waves break explosively behind us, while ahead, PARATII slices through the white foam of waves that broke just moments ago. As we are going along, the scale is growing. What were short, steep hills and valleys now become mountains and crevasses. In good weather, the waves are long and smooth. In strong winds, they become so tall I am certain my journey has been lengthened by all the climbs and descents.

With these ups and downs, my concern for icebergs changes. Few icebergs are visible, and I feel more comfortable with every new berg I see. It is relatively easy then to also locate its offspring—the true danger in these waves. Bergy bits can be as large as a two-story house, but they are almost invisible in the water, sometimes exposing no more than one foot of their mass above the waterline, not enough even as a resting spot for birds.

Speaking of birds, the quantity of birds in the area has increased, as well as the number of varieties, though albatross sightings are still very rare. I have trouble distinguishing between the various species of petrels; some look like natives from Kerguelen and Heard Islands, while others look like common species. Fulmar, Wilson, storm petrels, and cape pigeons—sometimes in droves—are easy to recognize. What an impressive talent these circumpolar beings have in their ability to find their way to home shores with such precision around the earth. No instruments, no charts . . . What a privilege it is for them to navigate the skies, high above these confused seas, the foam and noise upon which I have insisted on traveling. The noise may be the only element in common between those who travel on wings and those who travel under sail. The unending howling of the winds, and waves growing tall astern . . .

My concern with the height of the waves is soon replaced by my admiration for the amazing vistas every time PARATII rises to those mountain crests. Who said there are no majestic views on the high seas?

Average speeds are back to five degrees of longitude per day, after several days of tall but orderly seas. These good eastward gains end any remaining despondency and soothe any discomfort I might experience. The days with the heater turned on seem like centuries ago—and I don't miss them at all.

I must admit I am enjoying a bit of physical comfort in my routine, especially compared to that of crews of centuries past, who had to climb out onto the yards, clinging for dear life as they worked the sails of tall sailing ships. On the other hand, my comfort is offset by the white-knuckle stress of being all alone in managing and running the boat down here in this totally unpredictable environment of sporadic winds, sticky fog, and the devilish movement of icebergs, true renegades on the high seas.

The winds have finally shifted, turning westerly, pushing me in the right direction. Though strong at times, the wind doesn't manage to confuse the seascape. Visibility is much better, despite the sun's rare appearances. Traffic is as calm as Stockholm on a Sunday morning.

After I voiced all my doubts about its durability, the mast has earned my trust. Whenever it rotates it makes a grating sound internally, at the deck-level rotation ring. Perhaps the end of the boom shipped some water when PARATII dipped into a wave. An occasional dab of grease seems to mute the noise.

Up on deck the big question is about storm trysail procedures. I have started using it not only during gales, but also whenever I handle the mainsail, hoisting it on the lee side of the mainsail when raising it, and to the windward side when lowering it. There are no points given for heroics out here.

The noon positions, which I mark off daily as colored-pencil triangles on the large polar chart, are beginning to take the shape of a respectable snake. My beloved GPS has gradually replaced all other instruments. I now use it for countless functions in addition to determining our position—to control the batteries, calculate averages, time, distances, speeds, magnetic deviation—everything. The conventional instruments I have on board, excluding the wind speed indicator, have all been turned off in order to reduce the number of blinking lights on the control panel.

As we cruised along inside the Convergence, groups of islands whose archaic names reminded me of children's books fell behind. The Prince Edward Islands, Edward and Marion, separated by an 11-mile channel, were now behind me, three hundred miles to the north. Three days later, I passed another group at the same distance to the north, the Crozet Islands. Marion Dufresne discovered both groups in 1772. James Cook named them in 1776, at the end of his great voyage along the Atlantic Convergence, exploring the lands around the still "nonexistent" continent.

Cook was certainly one of history's greatest commanders and captains. The fact that he was so persistent and discovered so many unknown lands around Antarctica, without ever having discovered the largest of all, the continent itself, is a spectacular irony.

His third expedition which, as fate would have it, was to be his last voyage to Antarctica, carried a new instrument on board, a technological marvel that would forever change navigation and geography, John Harrison's chronometer.

The determination of longitude involves a calculation requiring the exact time—in hours, minutes, and seconds—relative to a specific reference point. This requirement was the single greatest navigational and cartographical brainteaser of the day, ultimately resolved by the invention of the mobile chronometer, first tested in 1762. Since 1772, Cook had carried a copy of that mechanism on his voyages aboard RESOLUTION. It was known simply as model K-1, built by Larcum Kendall. By combining the instrument's precision with his own skill, Cook achieved unprecedented success in his explorations. The *Antarctic Pilot*, an essential onboard guide for anyone who sails Antarctic waters, is a catalogue of Cook's discoveries and voyages around Antarctica.

The Kerguelen Islands, also explored by RESOLUTION in 1776, had been discovered only four years earlier by Yves Joseph Kerguelen-Tremarek, a discovery that was rooted in scandal. Young Kerguelen, whose fertile imagination got the best of him, described the islands as a giant tropical paradise beyond the possessions of Great Britain. This report won him commendations, and command of a second expedition. However, the truth was soon exposed, that the islands were utterly inhospitable because of stormy and freezing weather, and Kerguelen was court-martialed and sent to prison.

On Thursday, December 17, one hundred fifty miles north of my route, Kerguelen's new world falls away behind. Any temptation I might have to make a stop at the island group's main bay, Port-aux-Français, is abandoned after looking at the comparative weather tables of the Antarctic's stormiest islands. Whereas Grytviken averages 15 days per year of gale force winds—that is, winds of force nine or higher on the Beaufort scale— Port Lockroy has 36 days; Macquarie, 51 days, and Port-aux-Français averages 180 days per year of storms of that intensity!

"Thank you very much, but no. Good-bye, Kerguelen. See you another time!"

I have completed 4,000 miles within the Convergence—9,000 more to go. That's over one-quarter of the voyage, with average daily performance improving and PARATII in perfect shape. A small celebration in the galley for another 1,000 miles made good—then back to work. I take advantage of the reasonably light wind and clear weather to again invert the windvane autopilot lines. I write in my log, "Next line inversion in two weeks or 2,500 miles, whichever comes first." Then, I go to bed.

The next morning, Friday, I pass the last group of islands, the McDonald Islands (53°03'S and 72°31'E), two hundred thirty miles southwest of Kerguelen. This is a group of four islands, McDonald, Flat Island, Meyer Rock and, 23 miles west of those, Heard Island, the largest of the group. Heard Island is of recent volcanic formation (53°06'S and 73°31'E), and was sighted for the first time in November 1833 by British sealer Peter Kemp, aboard the brig MAGNET. In January 1971, the first humans to set foot on the island were scientists from the French oceanographic ship GALLIENI, stepping off a helicopter.

I want each stage to be highly visible, so I use colored pencils to fill in our position triangles on Chart No. 4009, our daily noon positions. There were twenty-three red triangles leading up to Kerguelen. From that point on I switched to orange-colored pencils until I complete the voyages' next major stage, crossing the International Date Line (Greenwich's ante meridian), an eternity from here.

Well, not really. Two more folds in my chart and I will be plotting positions in the Pacific Ocean. Once I put Australia behind me, the next land I will pass will be Australia's Macquarie Island. If everything runs smoothly I'll leave it to my north. Covering that stretch will account for 3,300 miles traveled inside the Convergence, with only 730 miles to go to reach 180° longitude—the Date Line. When distances between waypoints are so great, it makes sense to travel along a great-circle route (which involves changing headings constantly), rather than along a rhumb line (which follows a straight line drawn on the chart). There is a difference of 400 miles by sailing along a great-circle route, rather than sailing along a rhumb line. Such navigational and cartographical problems, minor on short voyages, are important now, especially using Mercator charts.

Geographical objectives sometimes seem far away—measured in miles, time zones, degrees of longitude, or declinations—but calendar events are a different story. Christmas is approaching at lightning speed, less than one week away. Shipbuilding activities at Itapevi, where PARATII's larger sister is slowly being born, have probably shut down. The Christmas spirit is already permeating

everyone's lives, in São Paulo and throughout the world. The twins
are learning to say *Babai Noel.*

In keeping with the Christmas spirit, I muster up the courage,
in the early hours of Saturday morning, to undertake a serious
housecleaning operation before the Department of Public Health
and Safety of the Southern Ocean shuts down the galley. With a
bucket, hot water and soap, pant legs and shirt cuffs rolled up, I
attack every inch of every tiny corner under the sink, behind the
stove, even underneath the floorboards. When I stand up again,
my back aches as I assume the pose of a housecleaner, hands on
my waist, elbow resting on the end of the mop stick.

I can't believe it. "This can't be the same boat!"

The stainless steel on the stove and heater gleam brightly. The
boat's interior smells of pine detergent. A rare show of order and
cleanliness. I can see my nose reflected on the stainless steel pans
as if I were in a house of mirrors. The previous night's gale has
turned into a calm; the constant fog has finally dissipated and,
free of clouds, the sun comes out.

At last, a completely blue sky without the slightest trace of
clouds, not a wisp of white anywhere. Not in the skies or on the
water. No clouds, no ice, no foam from waves—nothing but blue.
The wind is light and southerly. This Saturday will be filled with
nothing but sunshine. Albatrosses and giant petrels, bewildered
by the absence of wind, unable to fly, settle on the water just
inches away from PARATII. An errant albatross with a lot of white
on its wings, probably an elder, circles majestically several times
in flawless skimming maneuvers, the tips of its wings just millimeters above the water, perhaps showing off a bit for those already
in the water. There are zillions of cape pigeons. I see one albatross, a dark one this time, may be a sooty, and a petrel or two.
Who ever said this place is deserted, forgotten by God?

I know days like this are rare down here. In four weeks this is a first, and precisely the reason why I am enjoying each minute of daylight and heat, as if it was the most important day of my life onboard since leaving our little house in Jurumirim.

During these rare pleasant moments, I also summon the courage necessary for taking a bath; this will be my fourth. I turn on the heater—ah, hot water again. PARATII's pitching lost some of its violence, so I take advantage of the opportunity to shave and give myself a haircut. I put on new clothes, dry boots, and clean socks.

Wearing boots at all times, even while sleeping, caused the only problem with my lower extremities: cold feet. Thick socks do not keep feet warm. What keeps feet warm are well-ventilated boots. I do not have any more breathable inserts, so I custom make a pair, from dinner placemats made of perforated rubber. Success!

Of course I could take off my boots when I sleep, but I would never feel relaxed. If anything happened that called for an urgent dash on deck—like yesterday when the trysail sheet broke—the seconds lost putting on my boots could carry a high cost. It is a thousand times better, to sleep at the ready for such a dash, though I must say, it feels weird crawling into a sleeping bag, boots and all.

And my boots are on tonight, when spring is ending. Summer has begun. I am nine hours ahead of Brazil now, clean-shaven and in a clean house. But once again we are slicing through fog, and snow occasionally blows across the deck from the south.

From PARATII's own southern regions, the bilges, comes a new sound on board. Over the past few weeks, I have become a keen-eared noise hunter. But this isn't enough; I need to identify its source. A sailor's paranoia, you think? Maybe so. But no single noise bothers me as long as I know what is causing it. A bottle of olive oil slamming against a shelf in the galley, an oil can rolling in the bilges, the whining sound at the keel-stepped foot of the mast (not the same grating sound the mast was making at deck-level). The voices of rudder bushings, inaudible on deck, when heard from below remind me of old ladies gossiping excitedly. We have every imaginable sound on board.

I go down into the saloon, eavesdropping in the corners, pressing my ear against the bulkheads, gloves hanging from clenched teeth. I soon discover that the metallic, sporadic sound I am hearing comes from the famous junk box: two little stainless steel bars rolling from side to side every time a wave hit.

While I am locking the box back into place in the hold, using one hand to support myself against a shelf, my eyes fall on a new book, still unread. The title is *Saved*. It is a gift Júlio gave me months earlier, which for lack of time I have not yet opened. I pull the book out and go back up to the navigation table. I don't go back to sleep.

It is a bad idea to have opened that book. It is a survival story, the account of one of the most spectacular rescues ever made in the Southern Ocean, during the Vendée Globe singlehanded race around the planet, which ended last year.

The Vendée Globe is by far the longest and most impressive sporting challenge I know. Unfortunately, in Brazil, where we practice sports that are usually surrounded by fences, this type of event, whose race track is the planet itself, does not get much media coverage. The race tests endurance and skill not for a mere ninety minutes, as in soccer, but over four solid months, twenty-four hours a day, on the most sobering sports field of all, the Southern Ocean. I have always been fascinated with long events that test not only endurance, but also management, strategy, and respect for materials and the medium itself.

The race was run along a route that came very close to ours, some one hundred miles to the north, just shy of the Atlantic portion of the Convergence. *Saved* is the story of the spectacular rescue of Tony Bullimore, survivor of the *Exide Challenger*, who, coincidentally, capsized very near to my current position, at 100°E and 52°S. That year's race was particularly tragic. Raphael Dinelli, a young Frenchman, capsized and sank south of Australia, and was miraculously saved by England's Pete Goss in a smaller boat under dreadful sea conditions over Christmas of 1996. A few days later, Thierry Dubois and Bullimore capsized between Kerguelen and Macquarie, very close to each other, both surviving six days adrift in freezing waters, the Frenchman hanging on to his upturned rudder as waves crashed over him, and England's Bullimore, 60 years old and highly experienced, remained trapped in an air bubble inside his hull. There was yet another disaster in that race: Canadian Garry Roofs also capsized in the Pacific Ocean, and was lost at sea.

Now, I did not plan on reading about recent tragedies in waters so near, but I am unable to control my curiosity. The book describes waves that were six, seven, even eight-stories high; howling 60- and 70-knot winds—I cannot put the damn thing down. Is the English author exaggerating? I don't think so. Regardless, those descriptions of vile weather disturb me quite a bit, especially since I am sailing in the same area.

Most irritating is to read Bullimore praising, first the qualities of his boat, though it barely managed to surf those waves; and, second, his automatic pilot nicknamed Bertha which actually proved wholly incapable of holding a heading.

"Hell, a worthless contraption such as that doesn't deserve a nickname," I think.

Still, though I am mad at the author and the person who gave me the book, I cannot unglue myself from it. I have had several nightmares for which those pages are to blame. Only after having reached its end, much later, am I able to acknowledge that it was a very interesting and well-written book. It was also clear that Australia's SAR (search and rescue) services carried out that summer their most brilliantly executed operations ever.

Moved by what I have been reading of late, I decide to inspect every line on board, including sail seams and autopilot control lines. PARATII's old windvane autopilot, which had also been designed by Mr. Knoos, had been nicknamed Florence. She was flawless and indeed deserved her nickname. This time I think it best not to name anything, though it is clear that my new Sailomat is far superior to Bullimore's Bertha. Despite its poor construction and the fact that parts, bushings, and tabs are constantly falling off, it performs its duties under whatever sea conditions it encounters.

My own "Bullimore week" begins quickly on Christmas Day when I am pinching the southerlies to gain latitude. It's a euphemism to call it wind, that scandalous turbine of air jetting toward us from starboard, from the south. Twenty-four hours of gales, swearing and violence on a date that should be so peaceful, when only good thoughts should occupy our minds. Nevertheless, for better or worse, I have now completed two-fifths of the journey—5,000 miles—and my big red truck is still barreling eastward. Despite frequent gales, PARATII has not yet been reduced to bare poles; neither had she been forced to heave-to, that passive, escapist position I have always sought to avoid.

Christmas Day is spent in liquid disarray, under foggy and gray skies. I am not jumping for joy, nor am I much interested in a Christmas dinner and whatnot. The truth is I miss Marina and the twins, my two sisters, my crazy brother-in-law Wilson, and Cacá—I could just imagine them all, painting the town red. The girls from Nutrimental, Regina and Takako, prepared a Christmas dinner for me, with wines, sweets, presents and all, which they hid away, high in the galley cupboard. With the boat pitching so much, I can barely reach it. A piece of Parma ham hangs in the head next to the galley, swinging from side to side, sometimes hitting the ceiling.

As the night wears on, I am losing all hope of enjoying any peace at all when, as if by divine and inexplicable decree, the winds die and the sea turns flat as a swimming pool. Rather than go to bed in a self-pitying funk, I spring from the tube on which the bunk was slung, turn on the galley lights, and kick off a party that lasts until the wee hours of the next morning. Sérgio, of the CASO SÉRIO, gave me a tiny fake Christmas tree that requires some assembly, its various parts stowed in a film can. I assemble the tree and place it over the electronic autopilot. I find an Italian fruit cake, unspeakably delicious, a gift from Fábio Tozzi. The wines from the girls in Curitiba and the champagne Marina gave me—I decide to save those until the day I step on dry land again. Drinking around here is impossible. Besides, with the way the boat suddenly stopped rolling, the burning incense, and smoke from candles I have lit—I have more than enough buzz going already.

I look at my watch: almost midnight. What an unexpected mood reversal! Wow! If only I could hear the girls' little screams, the sounds they must be making right now!

It has been days since I managed a decent radio contact with Brazil. What if I tried to point the Inmarsat antenna manually? At 5:00 a.m., after numerous attempts, the gizmo makes contact with the satellite. Brazil is nine hours behind me, which means they are still enjoying Christmas Eve dinner.

I speak with everyone. The girls are screaming, the blonde keeps running away while the brunette tries to say, "Babai, baco! Babai, baco! [Daddy, boat!]. What a great Christmas present, their little voices, 9,000 miles from home. Zé Montanaro and Sílvia are at the beach. Everyone is celebrating—and it is still *last* night. It occurs to me that, if I had a newspaper around here, I could give them tomorrow's news. But there are no news to give, really. I am just homesick, with a powerful desire to make the remaining longitudes fly by.

8

THE NEW YEAR AT MY BACK

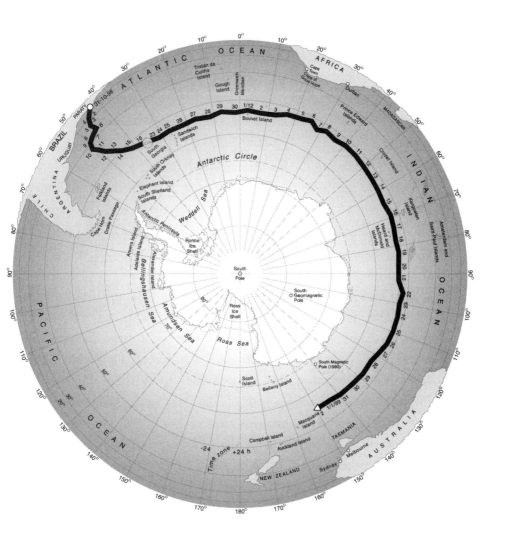

Not a single wish did you ever have that was not my own
Such was the craziness I felt over you that,
As I felt you becoming ever more mine,
I was becoming ever more yours.

———————

Lost behind the cupboard *O Messidor* by Guilherme de Almeida. A bookseller gave me the book long ago, though I have no idea how it found its way into that hiding spot. I prefer a thousand times over to read of suffering in my own language than of courage in a foreign tongue. My reading problems are getting worse—hardly any Portuguese books remain. I can't bear any accounts about the cold and heroic feats written in English. In addition to navigation, I have every other manual as well: instrument and electronics, cookbooks, and manuals for things I already know how to do. This is my working library, which was organized and placed on a shelf along the low inner wall of the navigation table. The books I like most, now reduced to only a few, made their way up the steps to the pilothouse, earning a spot on the floor in an orange-colored box within easy reach, near my feet.

Something is wrong with the weather; a sudden change in temperature and wind. Perhaps it is the Convergence line, which in these parts reaches far south toward the Ross Sea, dipping toward us again. Also, birds that had been constantly present are now gone, and new ones begin to appear, like small brown petrels flying in the thousands, but never approaching the boat.

———

Magnetic deviation is dropping abruptly these days, an indicator that the magnetic and geographic poles are rapidly falling into alignment. When the magnetic deviation shifts from west to east, I will finally be able to celebrate having passed the longitude of the magnetic South Pole.

The magnetic poles, North and South, toward which all regular compass needles point, are actually quite removed from the geographic poles, and are constantly, albeit slowly, shifting. My latest data on the position of the magnetic South Pole, taken from Chart No. 4074, placed it at 65°S and 139°E, in the middle of the ocean, 900 miles from the true South Pole. Regardless, it is too early to be thinking of celebrating passing the pole, be it magnetic or true.

Almost 1,200 miles south of Australia, the main celebration during this festive season is summarized in a log entry, for some reason written in red: "We have reached Australia." The island that I have always wanted to visit is just a little over 1,000 miles north of PARATII's position. But I have no desire to stop there now, not in Tasmania or anywhere else. To do so would only mean I had to stop, that I gave up on my voyage. The farther south I can go with the wind's help, the shorter my path, in time and distance, to our next landfall, Dorian Bay. Macquarie Island, the nearest land to my intended route, is a full week away.

Sunday, December 27. Under full sail, which happens rarely, I am having British tea and biscuits, my feet propped up on the control panel, which would have embarrassed any well-mannered Briton. The biscuits are on my lap, the teacup in my hand, when ... I almost toss all against the ceiling. A gust of wind brings PARATII on her side in a flash. The pulverized biscuits start flying all over the place while I run out on deck.

"Lower the mainsail and raise the storm trysail!" Orders shouted, orders obeyed—in seconds.

The barometer is low and the weather depressing; I feared a surprise like this. The boom is let out to 90 degrees; sail area reduced as much as possible and sheeted home.

PARATII is running through the waves as if they, too, were biscuits. But these biscuits are getting bigger and bigger. One comes up from astern and engulfs us. When the foam finally blows off the deck I am pleased to see the windvane still in one piece.

Tuesday, December 29. The barometer needle, falling dramatically, hit the hygrometer arm which is already off the scale. Things keep getting worse. The tiny storm trysail cannot be reduced any further. My only option would be to remove it, but then I would have less rudder and speed with which to run the mountainous following seas. I reduce the jib to the size of an umbrella. Even so, PARATII is making over twelve knots . . . eighteen . . . twenty . . . even twenty-two knots. Oh God! Every time she surfs downhill I look around for a brake pedal. There is none.

The sharp grating sounds coming from the engine room turn into alarming screams. The brake! There *is* a brake on board. On the propeller shaft there is a brake to prevent the propeller from spinning by the force of the water alone and then damage the transmission. At these high speeds, with PARATII surfing down waves, the water pressure on the propeller is so great that the braking mechanism slipped, producing an awful whining sound. I tighten the brake pads as much as I can and go back up to the pilothouse. I transfer the helm from the Swedish autopilot to the electronic one, which is easier to disengage if I run into any problems holding our heading.

Every time a wave explodes, it leaves foam surrounded by clear turquoise rings. The water has a milky color that could only be the result of extreme pressure. I have never seen seas like these.

This morning in the galley I sorted all the ingredients for the day's menu: my lucky gnocchi for the 29th, with placemats and everything. But the gnocchi didn't have a chance. I am unable to pull myself away from the observation deck or from the helm, even for a second. I am mesmerized. The package of gnocchi flew to the floor and is tossed back and forth. With it are the cutting board, the Parmesan shredder, a soup bowl, a gourd from the *Ver o Peso* [Watch the Weight] market in Belém, and knives and spoons. One of the drawers opens, spilling its contents down the galley hallway. The Bosch drill charger slams against a bulkhead and explodes into fragments.

Thirty minutes before midnight, local time. The situation: bad—it cannot get any worse. Outside, a hellish darkness. The only thing I can see is PARATII's wake and spray across the surface of the water, both illuminated by heavy phosphorescence. It has been hours since I last ate anything. My hands are glued to the helm.

I notice some improvement but do not comment on it, so I start to work on that lucky meal—though I don't believe in luck. Out of the boiling water, somehow or another, I manage to extract an almost raw gnocchi, which I eat in silence at the navigation table. My eyes are glued to the anemometer. Forty, forty-five, fifty knots! With the boat's speed, the apparent wind adds another twelve to fifteen knots. In other words, at least sixty knots of utter chaos. Sometimes it seems to drop a bit, but then another gust hits. The wind generator emits a desperate moan louder than the wind. I manage to turn it off without having to go out on deck.

Any sleep I get comes while seated at the control panel. I dare not venture below, even to wash the dishes. I pray that the boat will not broach in the middle of this pandemonium, I will not run into icebergs or anything else up ahead, and that nothing will break. The hours drag on while I am getting increasingly sleepy. I dream of sleeping, but lack the courage to abandon my watch, even for a second.

The final day of the year begins with the seas still out of control. The barometer has now been off the scale for over fifty hours, and shows no sign of rising again. I have completely lost any notion of what normal means. The sun peeks out occasionally, only to reveal daytime sights more frightening than the scariest moments of windy horror at night. The entire surface of the sea is covered with milky white and turquoise water. The apparent wind has dropped to thirty-five or forty knots, yet the waves are more menacing than ever.

The churning seas, stretching forever around me, distort my perception of space. I am no longer sailing east, north, or south, but straight up and straight down. Sometimes a cliff appears from the north as a precipice forms to the south. Perhaps these are not waves at all, but liquid holes, valleys traveling the seas. Who knows? Incredibly my little boat is behaving in a rather dignified manner. She slips sideways, burying the entire boom in water, then immediately rights herself and resumes her course without my ever having to take the helm. My fingers, just millimeters from the wheel, ready to disengage the autopilot or make an abrupt course correction, never need to touch it.

While I am hoping for the weather to improve, the seas actually worsen. Before high noon (the sun must have been out there somewhere), the GPS magnetic deviation indicator jumps from west to east. PARATII just passed the longitude of the magnetic South Pole (the alignment between the geographic and magnetic Poles only happens twice in a South Pole circumnavigation).

Coincidentally, the odometer on that same GPS shows exactly 9,000 miles made good since Jurumirim, and 6,479 miles since I said good-bye to Harold and Hedel in Grytviken.

To top things off, a little while later I cross 140°E longitude, which I interpret as the official end of the Indian Ocean, the end of the world, and precisely at the end of the year. The only reason my mood stays upbeat is that just yesterday I crossed the ante-meridian to our home, our beloved little ramshackle house under the coconut trees of Jurumirim. Now, every second of forward progress and every mile made good will bring me closer to Paraty. (The antemeridian for Jurumirim sits on 44°40W longitude, is 135°20'E, the exact opposite side of the earth, 180 degrees away).

During those fifty or sixty hours of fierce gale, the farthest point on the voyage is left astern. This doesn't ease our immediate situation in the least, but just knowing that the distance remaining is now less than the distance already covered, that half of the circumnavigation and half of my long-held dream are now completed are—despite the sea, the fear, and the weather—one hell of a reason to party. A party on the other side of the world, Antarctica, the geographic and magnetic Poles, farther away than ever. I will now be closing in on home and those I love.

We passed through the Indian Ocean, and made all calculations and considerations about longitudes and distances, and the year 1998 is gone as well. Watching the sunset and a full moon, twelve hours ahead of the folks back home, I usher in the New Year searching for excuses to celebrate.

In my naïveté, I assume that the barometer's return to scale on such an important date is the harbinger of the storm's end. Who knows? Maybe from here on we'll have good weather and pleasant seas . . .

Radio propagation has been zilch for some time, and the telephone refuses to complete calls. There is no way to speak with Brazil. My only privilege will be to kick off the New Year before everyone else back home. After so much wind, there is nothing outside but ice-cold surface foam. No albatrosses, petrels, sea-gulls—nothing. The strange and milky color of the stirred-up seas transfers to the sky now, which is now growing darker; and the final sunset of the year is the strangest yet.

New Year's morning comes, with Macquarie Island 536 miles ahead, and the Date Line, 1,244 miles. This is not exactly what I would most like to see at the start of a new year, not a day that looks like this. I have my doubts about the weather, but even more ominously, the barometer, which promised to rise, drops again. Again the apparent winds begin to hit fifty knots.

Resigned, as if bad weather were the only possible kind, I furl what is left of the jib. We will keep only the small storm trysail as our single sail. Single? More like widowed.

And then the Southern Ocean unleashes its full fury. Any levity or good mood vanishes. The ounces of patience spent trying to understand what is happening are soon exhausted. Complete chaos—a nonstop, out-of-control apocalypse of water and foam. The seas are imploding around us.

I failed to notice that the sheet to the storm trysail, the only engine driving PARATII at totally illegal speeds, has been chafing against a block. Now it threatens to snap. If the slightest piece of cloth breaks loose, or if the sheet breaks, a spectacular disaster is awaiting us.

I build up my courage, cut a piece of line, go outside, and inch like an octopus along the boom to rig a backup sheet, praying the whole time that a wave will not rip me off the boom. I sure could use four extra limbs.

The sixteen-millimeter line is flailing in the wind like a thin wool thread. It is no fun at all making turns and tying knots while dangling out over the sea foam. Instead of speaking in a loud voice, I yell. I shout orders to myself. I shout that the knot is not tight enough. I yell to hear my own voice in the midst of the hellish sounds of that unstoppable wind. I yell to keep my strength from waning, refusing to give up before I have tied every necessary knot.

I go below. Miraculously, I am not drenched. Using a heavy

black terrycloth towel I dry myself—clothes, foul-weather jacket, pants, boots, and all.

Minutes later, a side-swiping waterfall rolls in from the north and smacks PARATII's stern just as we are surfing down a wave from the west. She broaches. The galley rises and the navigation table drops. While I am still holding the towel, I slide across the sole and slam into the far wall. Outside, the boom, where I was just moments ago, plunges into the wave. The trysail is flapping wildly, desperately waiting for the autopilot to regain control.

"You're taking too long. You're taking too long," I shout. I turnoff the autopilot and take over the internal helm. My God, this is even worse. The boat righted herself but I cannot hold her course because I have no reference points. Looking forward, I can't tell if the waves we are surfing are rolling in from the north or the west. To steer by compass is not the solution either.

So I turn my back to the bow and, watching the waves astern, holding the helm behind my back, I discover that I can steer by watching the walls of waves and the windvane on the stern arch. Surfing backwards! Who would have thought! This is certainly not the way I planned to start the year. My New Year's resolutions have been reduced to just one: get out of here alive.

9

A BOAT YOU CAN
JUMP START

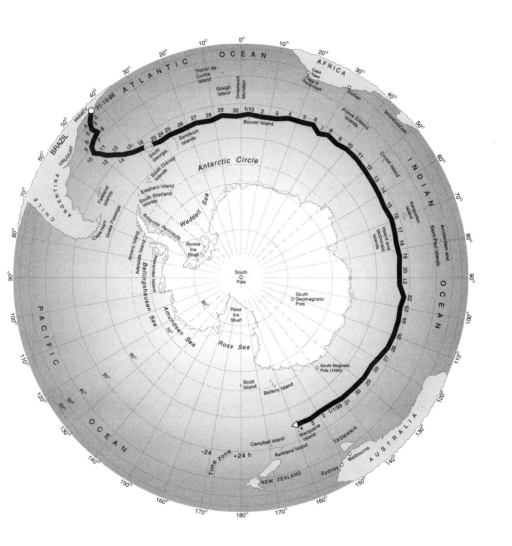

Saturday morning, January 2. "Thank you, thank you, thank you for being in one piece," I keep repeating. Friday's coffee, which flew into the air and ended up behind the radar screen at the back of the navigation table, is rolling back out now, staining the ship's log. I don't care as I watch the cold liquid draw dark spots on my chart. I am so happy that the wind has weakened, that the autopilot is working again. I am drinking coffee—fresh, piping hot coffee—while I am writing.

The seas are still chaotic but bearable now. PARATII survived without any breakdowns. I lost the indestructible windvane board that my friend Feijó in Guarujá built for me. I had transferred the helm over to the electronic autohelm until I got the chance to replace the board with a new one. I draw up an inspection list for all the lines and a list of future precautions.

What a great boat I have, a dear and valiant boat. Of course, I admire racing boats, the nautical versions of Formula One. Instead of racing around buoys, they race around the globe. But even those highly colorful machines that slice through oceans are hardly more efficient than my big red aluminum truck is in these higher latitudes. Actually, since PARATII entered the Convergence 40 days ago she has maintained average speeds that few plastic boats could maintain without risking getting impaled on the ice. PARATII is not just a machine. She was my—our house in Paraty. And "our house" is flying along at 55° latitude, 1,000 miles south of Australia.

We leave Tasmania behind, 720 miles to the north. Standing outside, without those damned mountaineering gloves, I hold onto the wooden handrail over the companionway. The wind from astern—still blowing 25 knots apparent—blows my hair to my face and into my eyes. It is wonderful to feel the sun again. It is wonderful to be done with that storm, the fiercest I've ever faced. It is wonderful to have a strong boat and not to have made many mistakes. It occurs to me that in almost 10,000 miles of rough sailing under this new mast I cannot remember a single *distribil*, as they say in Brittany—a sudden harrowing moment in which everything imaginable goes wrong, sails torn to shreds, lines tangled, crashes, jolts, breakdowns. We had none of the above. Oh, I've suffered the occasional cold fingers whenever I went out to make course adjustments—but that's it. I've adapted to the cold and to a routine of precautions aimed at preventing accidents, especially domestic accidents.

Other than her new experimental mast, PARATII was never modified. She is ten years old now, but I never had to deal with remodeling, maintenance, changes to systems or rigging, or even electronics. PARATII is not a fancy super yacht.

Her rudder system is flawless. It is totally simple, precise, reliable, and plainly solid; it has never been altered since it was installed. She has the same engine she's always had, which serves to charge batteries, activate the pumps, make water, and everything else, and runs as smoothly as a sewing machine. The engine has an optional manual ignition for complete peace of mind down in these climes where batteries get cold and lazy. Oh, and the batteries—nickel cadmium alkaline—can withstand all the modern demands of electric consumption. Despite PARATII's simple design, she is elegant, clean, and comfortable.

The new mast had been her only modification. And what a wonderful revolution it brought with it. Tons of tackle and hardware have become superfluous, and are now long gone. Fábio ended up using much of the discarded hardware on his boat,

BRISA, or on many boats on which he performed his mind-boggling surgeries. The only thing I really miss is the steel back-stay and shrouds, not as mast supports, unnecessary now that I have a carbon fiber mast standing free as a coconut tree. Rather, I miss the convenience of having them as handholds when I run up and down the deck. With the shrouds and stays gone, crossing PARATII's deck can prove quite a challenge in heavy seas, whereas before I could use them as stepping stones to help me keep my balance.

The lifelines are high, but not high enough to keep a distracted mariner from flying overboard. Any drunkard or visitor who will insist on walking on only two feet faces a short lifespan, or at least a quick trip into the sea. An unexpected benefit that came with the new mast is that I can climb onto the flat-topped boom to perform tasks or just enjoy the ride, with less risk than being on deck, even with the boom swung way out from the boat. And at seven feet above the deck I am high and dry, well protected from any waves that might choose to sweep the deck or swamp the boat.

During the long hours of the day the corner where the boom meets the mast has become my favorite location. Leaning against the sail, I admire the waves passing below, washing the deck without getting myself wet. Sometimes the boom will strike a large wave and rotate, but movement at the center of rotation—where I am cozily nestled—is minimal and safe. Now, I sit in this observation post, scrunched up and with my gloves on, watching the sea fall away behind us. I am exhausted. I have lost count of the days of bad weather and successive lows. The white wake we are leaving behind blends in with the froth of the waves, which are still formidable. The seas are hard and angular, and PARATII's heavy rolling keeps her from surfing down the waves, which are decreasing in size.

There is no reason to feel heroic or to celebrate; yet, exhausted as I am, I feel hugely relieved that everything is over for now. I have a burning desire to tell someone that everything is okay. I want so badly to have someone ask me, "How was your New Year?"

"New Year? Parties? Come here, I'll show you my New Year!" I bellow into the wind.

Any pagan would have good reason to pray after seeing those seas. But this is no place to be praying, there is still too much work to do. Enough laziness! I jump from my white post and run back inside. In good time too, because I can no longer feel my fingers or my nose, that's how cold they are.

There is no way to communicate with Brazil. Propagation is not cooperating and all electronic means of communication have decided to remain silent. I could make contact through Australia if I wanted to, but I decide to wait a few more days.

On Sunday I pass the longitude line that marks the easternmost tip of Australia, Cape Byron. I hope I'll never need to pass this way again under similar conditions. Since December 26, PARATII never rested, not for a second. Her every nerve have been stretched; even my nerves have almost been destroyed. My eardrums hurt. Just then, for the hundredth time, the propeller drive shaft starts spinning. Even the brake pads are worn out! The engine room has the burnt-rubber smell of a bobtail truck riding its brakes down the mountain from São Paulo to Santos!

The surprise of the day happens during one of the final surfing descents of the watch, when the drive shaft, screaming from down below, once again breaks loose and starts spinning. Now, I don't know how this happened, but as we surf to the bottom of the wave, the engine turns over and starts.

"That's impossible! Who turned on the engine?"

With the drive shaft screaming and the motor running at top

speed, I run aft. The throttle is in the "forward" position. I put it in "neutral," go inside, and pulls the choke. There, it stops! Unbelievable. This is the first time I'd ever seen a boat start by popping the clutch. There are no ghosts around, no signs of empty bottles on board. The only explanation must be that I unknowingly stepped on the lever that activates the gearbox, and during one of our surfing descents the force of the water turned the drive shaft, and the engine kick-started. Because the diesel cutoff is mechanical, the starter worked even without the electronic ignition.

"Perhaps this is a sign that *everything* is going to work," I joke. And decide to get the Inmarsat telephone to work, too.

Two hours later there are three little stars on the device. I managed to connect with the satellite stationed over the Pacific Ocean.

"Miserable gadget, talk to me! Talk to me!" I shout, pressing the keypad.

And it talks. Marina's voice, crystal clear on the voice message system at home. Damn, no one is home. I call Paraty and find everyone at Wilson's house. My sisters are there, as well as my screaming twins. Marina tells me everyone was worried. She asks if I know what happened in Tasmania, in the Sydney-Hobart regatta. Of course, all I know is that my body is aching from banging into things for the past full week.

Last Saturday, December 26, four hours before the Sydney start of one of the three most famous regattas in the world, a gale warning was issued. In the midst of pre-race festivities and Saturday's glorious sunshine, the warning was largely ignored. By Monday morning 115 boats had been damaged, seven had sunk, and six men had died, swept by waves up to twenty-five meters high! It was the other side of the same depression that caught PARATII further to the south. It was the largest tragedy in the 54-year history of the Sydney-Hobart Race.

My father used to say, sarcastically, that ignorance is bliss. I have to agree. If anyone had told me, or if a bulletin had fallen into my hands describing the severity of that depression, I would have spent the year-end holidays in total panic.

I refuse to worry about my bank balance and stay on the phone, burning up cash to the tune of ten dollars a minute. I don't know when I will ever get a connection again, so I start calling friends and family.

I have a shouting conversation with Barba at his cozy restaurant in São Paulo, *Giordano*. My friend Quartim at the bank shouts his greetings in the traditionally outrageous manner of our family, of which he is an honorary member. I take a chance and call the village of Bik Faya in Lebanon, where I find my dear Uncle Ghassane, Aunt Tamara, and cousin Zeina, at home, sitting by their fireplace. I yell, "Merry Christmas!" They cry and then shout "Happy New Year!" I cry too. It is neither a logical nor particularly useful conversation, but it is the best thing that could happen to me these days. I speak with Jaime Pasmanik, my friend Bráulio's father, and wish him a happy birthday even though it is a month late.

All the yammering drains the batteries, so I have to start the engine. When the calls end, I watch the sun go down in the west, on a sea as smooth as a first-press Italian olive oil. It is the same sea, but it looks like another planet. Who would believe such a transformation is possible?

With the energy boost the phone calls produced, I wash four more pairs of socks, a hated but vital operation. I used my new boots only once, but they are already goners. As was another pair of new boots. They are size twelve, and I wear size eleven, but with my socks on, they are just too tight and uncomfortable as hell. Boots that don't allow air to circulate simply will not work. Size thirteen boots are just perfect. I have only one pair of that size, a gift from Hermann. These boots survived the old RAPA NUI days. It is the best pair of all, though the rubber is in such poor shape I know they won't last much longer, either.

This brief calm quickly returns life to normal. When we pass Macquarie Island, 75 miles to the north, the barometer suddenly spikes upward; the seas grow heavy and the winds strong. But this spike contains nothing, not by a long shot, to compare it with what I witnessed at year-end. I become shameless and switch to "survival mode" on board, using only the storm trysail, all other sails tightly furled. Nevertheless, with only minimal sail, we are able to keep up with our average speeds, covering five to six degrees of longitude daily.

At 56° S latitude, with shorter distances separating the longitudinal meridians, I complete another stage of my journey. I have two stages left. The next will be to cross the Date Line. Then, the final stage: 3,300 miles to the Peninsula, where I will anchor amid the rocks of Dorian Bay and the smelly Papua penguin guano. I am still a long way from *terra firma*, a long way. New Zealand is six hundred fifty miles to our north. We will pass near one last piece of land before reaching the Antarctic Peninsula: Campbell Island, two hundred fifty miles above our route. Actually, the nearest land to us is the land below our keel. The depth around here rose from almost 5,000 meters to a few hundred meters, indicating our arrival over the Macquarie Ridge, the platform on which the island sits and possibly the continuation of the trans-Antarctic mountain chain that begins in the Andes, on the other side of Antarctica and works its way over to a point almost above New Zealand. These are personal geological conclusions that make sense when you study charts of the ocean floor.

The small island to our north, Macquarie, forty-six square miles in size, is outside the Convergence, yet has a sub-Antarctic climate. It was discovered in 1810 by sealer captain Frederick

Hasselborough of the brig PERSEVERANCE. Within ten years, the island's seals were exterminated. Fourteen years later, its elephant seals met the same fate. The most notable ship to visit the island's unsheltered shores was the AURORA. Her last visit was in 1916–1917, as a support vessel to Shackleton's expedition, though she never made it to the Ross Sea. AURORA wintered on the island as she awaited Shackleton's group, which presumably was crossing Antarctica by land but was actually shipwrecked on the far side of the continent. She was ripped from the ice of McMurdo Sound, at Cape Evans, by a storm, and tossed out to sea. She drifted, abandoned, for ten months and 1,100 miles, like a MARY CELESTE—a ghost ship—until another ship found her and brought her back to Antarctica. Ernest Wild, brother of Frank Wild, Shackleton's right hand man, was one of ten men still on the island AURORA had abandoned. Those heroes, forgotten by history, would be saved much later by Shackleton himself. His feat, measured in effort and courage, was much greater than all of Scott's voyages combined. AURORA's anchor, with its severed chain, is still visible in the ground a few meters from the cabin that sheltered Scott on Cape Evans.

10

CROSSING THE DATE LINE

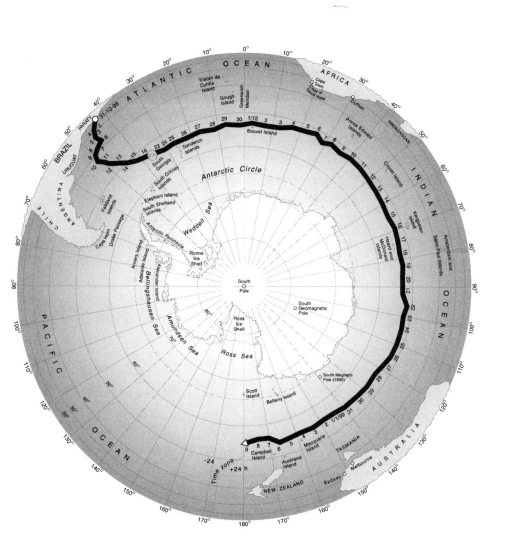

There was no need for dessert after the *fusili a carbonara* that Takako had prepared; it was that good. I gather the plates and silverware and, not being in the mood to wash dishes, I set everything down in the sink. Now this is a rare event: in the middle of the day, to return to my captain's chair armed with a cup of piping hot coffee held in my naked hands so I can feel the heat and enjoy the aroma. Oh, what was a delicious lunch that was!

It is too bad that while the seas are not heavy, valleys constantly cross the bow and cause the boat to stall—just as I am counting down the few miles left to arrive at the Date Line. It is obvious that something big has been happening. The barometer is still bouncing erratically and, on the radio, I hear Australians chattering nonstop about "pretty nasty weather down there . . ." and about the damage caused by the storm. But I haven't noticed anything yet. The only thing I want is to travel faster, cross the Date Line, be finished with the Pacific Ocean, and step ashore again at Dorian Bay.

Radio propagation opens up for the first time in the Pacific Ocean. Perhaps it is just a window, but I use it and enjoy a great conversation with everyone on our trusted old frequency. I speak with Hermann at his office, and with Fábio. My friend and accountant, Ulisses, PY2UAJ, coordinates communications at the other end. Júlio and Stickel are headed to Ushuaia by plane, where they will board KOTIC for their descent to Antarctica. A suitcase full of correspondence and gifts is already on its way; we need only to agree on a location. We will attempt a rendezvous and, if that fails, they will leave the suitcase for me to pick up when I arrive.

Despite headwinds, sea valleys, and my desire to increase speed, it takes us five days to cover the seven hundred miles lying between Macquarie Island in the western hemisphere and the Greenwich antemeridian. On Saturday, at 10:04 p.m. local time, 8:04 a.m. in Brazil, I cross the Date Line. We are back in our own hemisphere and that much closer to home.

West in view, halfway through! In an instant, while humming silly ditties, I get back to Friday, January 8. And one hour and fifty-six minutes later, Saturday, January 9, begins all over again. My weekend contains two Saturdays—January 9, twice in a row, and it is raining cats and dogs on both days. Now, instead of being fourteen hours ahead of Brazil time, I am ten hours behind! And rather than moving ever farther away in time, I am drawing closer!

That simple detail, duly noted in the log, is all it takes to lift my spirits and put a sparkle back into the dishes.

The brightest sparkles, however, come from the outside. With great difficulty because the wind insists on blowing from Antarctica down below, I tack southward to 57°S latitude. The next low rolls in from the west, and the waves grow tall again. PARATII is surrounded by heavy phosphorescence.

It is a dark night, the skies gray and moonless. PARATII's foamy wake glows brighter than ever before. Every movement of foam produces bright green flakes and crystals. Even the walls of the waves, far below their crests, take on a starry appearance that makes it difficult to distinguish black sky from sea. It is like sailing through outer space, surrounded by stars and comets. No matter how many times I've seen these displays, they always affect me strongly; I am lost in the three-dimensional glitter. The waves need not be very high, either, to produce the effect. I have seen the same phenomenon in Paraty, from the front door of our house, in the very calm waters of our little bay. There, it is not the crests of waves that generate the phosphorescence, but rather fish, darting this way and that, reacting to various sounds such as an outboard motor or canoe oars slicing softly through the water.

The simple act of returning to the western hemisphere turns my mind toward Jurumirim, still so far away. It is amazing to think that, though it has no electricity, that little place casts so much light on my ideas. There is a generator, an invention of Hermann's, used for minor repairs to the house or for drilling holes in wood. We rarely crank it up. But I don't want electric power, the real thing, ever to reach that house. We've gotten by without electricity for years, why would we need it now?

It's difficult to explain to an urban dweller the pleasure of sleeping with crickets, reading with a lantern, using torches to hunt for crabs, and making bonfires with driftwood the sea brought onto the beach. No neighbors' lights shine nearby, no telephone poles, no city noises or car sounds—and still we are so close to everything.

As luck would have it, not even the ubiquitous cellular phones stand a chance in Jurumirim. To get a signal you must row out a long way from the beach to the entrance to the bay, accessible only by canoe because there are no roads to take you there. And to receive a call? Forget it. If you have technology and funds, you're better off investing in your boat, not in the house.

Perhaps this is why we like it there so much. You can see so much more at night in a place that has no lights. I can't explain it.

PARATII was born in Jurumirim, in that lopsided and ramshackle house. She was born of conversations with people on other boats who sailed in from afar seeking shelter and water. I spoke to them of my longing to travel far away someday, to build a boat that is simple and strong, like our little house is.

I have planted lots of trees there, and Hermann has planted even more than I. Even the twins plant trees there. Some have withered, but many have grown, having figured out a way to co-exist with the surrounding wild vegetation. The result is a garden crafted into a landscape designed by nature herself. I hate high-rise buildings, mansions, swimming pools!

It takes a lot of sailing to learn to identify and appreciate a natural harbor. It is worth the time and effort of spending years at sea, making landfalls, and coasting along hostile and deserted shorelines to acquire an appreciation for green, sheltered, and well-situated harbors that offer a beautiful view.

I am baffled by the fact that we have lost the ability to recognize and appreciate natural harbors. In the past, Paraty was a one-of-a-kind harbor, unlike any other in the world. It was built because someone was able to recognize the true vocation of that little town—the sea. Life and the economy prospered in Paraty, thanks to the sea and the harbor. Mariners of yesteryear, infinitely more competent at identifying and appreciating good harbors, had to pick their way along the coast after sailing huge distances, then ease into untouched bays using rudimentary technology and a sharp look-out, in search of safe shelter.

Today, from way out here in the Pacific Ocean, I salute that special harbor in front of my old house. That's something else they knew how to do back then: how to choose a site for building a house, lay a foundation, use strong materials, and design solid architecture. In my time spent crawling around rocks while showing off to girlfriends, making my way through trails, and searching for old houses, I have come to understand how much knowledge we have "unlearned" as a result of our urban lives surrounded by concrete and asphalt—and how much I learned by having lived in Paraty.

In a hundred years, today's office buildings, apartment buildings, and condominiums will disappear. No longer will they shelter or employ anyone. Shoddy and egocentric constructions will go to ruin. And no one will travel from afar to visit them. But the pristine shores of Jurumirim will always draw visitors from around the globe.

If there is a single endeavor that deserves respect and investment, it is this: the conservation of harbors and shorelines. We need harbors where leisure holds sway over commerce, landscape over development, and service over infrastructure. Such harbors will have floating piers, ensuring that shorelines suffer as little impact as possible. My simple house in Jurumirim, invisible from the sea, still does not have (but soon will) a floating dock—discreet and careful in the way it touches the shore, as it should be. One need only travel by boat to understand why this is so important.

It was by traveling far, sometimes with no particular objective other than to see things that were once but are no more that I learned to enjoy places I had never cared much for, such as Rio de Janeiro.

By habit, we always seem to talk about Rio's beaches, which are nothing but sand deposits, unremarkable except for the crowds that exhaust the southward-facing beaches, oblivious to the spectacular convergence of forest, rock, and sea to the north.

Guanabara Bay was what brought this city into being, though it is now filthy and abused. I like to imagine what those men who discovered that stunning bay must have thought when they first sailed there, seeking shelter for their ships. I like to imagine what a beautiful place it could be again someday, under the protection of a conservation plan that would dredge out its depths to make it more navigable, rather than shrinking its size through landfill development projects. I like to imagine it as a safe harbor for sailboats and cruise ships that tie up on hundreds of arms of floating piers extending outward from the port, reviving the city's ancient piers and returning them to their rightful place in the life of the city.

As I am ruminating on ports and other dreams unlikely to become reality anytime soon, I get a jolt from one of those technological inventions that take your breath away. I have never used a pager before, and I hardly know how it works. When I left Brazil, I brought two telephones with me. One is the fixed Inmarsat. The second is a beta-test Iridium phone that was awaiting a new circuit board. With the Iridium telephone I was also given a pager. It, too, operates by satellite. The telephone that had been beta-tested in Brazil is merely a prototype. It would only become functional after I switched out the device's circuit board—as soon as I placed my hands on that suitcase being sent from Brazil. But the tiny pager is a fully functional product. And suddenly it has begun to work.

Revolutionary! It is impossible to describe the euphoria I feel when I hear the beeping sound, followed by a message from home, a message sent by one of my crazy friends, just seconds ago, from almost 10,000 miles away. I have no way to print the messages. I figure they'll soon fill up the 200-message memory, so I begin transcribing them, one by one, on sticky-note pads. These notes, in turn, invade the boat's control panel, and then begin to take over the pages in the logbook. News about the twins; the slow construction of my new boat in Itapeví; weather forecasts; useful radio frequencies; the position of lows headed my way; data on waves, wind, and currents; barometric pressure—you name it. Brazil is in yet another economic crisis, they're talking about new currency again, a new monetary circus. . . . Sometimes when reading a message I can recognize the voice of the person who sent it, just by the way it was written. My squalid, funny, and faithful friend Ronaldo, whom we nicknamed Tigrão, sent message No. 20:

DEAR AMYR, THANKS FOR THE CALL, IT WAS EXCITING TO
HEAR LIVE NEWS. CONGRATULATIONS ON THE 2/3 OF THE
TRIP. GOOD LUCK AMYYYYYR!!!
18:24 1/12/99 TIGRÃAAAO

Message No. 18 is from Marina:

FORECAST 24:00—HEAVY SEAS. FAVORABLE CURRENT. WAVES
25 TO 35 FT. WINDS 20 TO 45 KNOTS. IMPORTANT MAINTAIN
LATITUDE 57° — WINDS, CURRENT FAVORABLE.
    KISSES. MARINA. GOOD LUCK.
22:07 1/12/989 Y/ FAVORITE MARINA

While I am engaged in futuristic thoughts about Rio de Janeiro,
I receive another message, No. 15, from my father-in-law Mário, a
carioca [a Rio native]. His message reveals our forgetfulness.

HEY! AMYR! THE GALEÃO AIRPORT IS NOW THE ANTONIO
CARLOS JOBIM AIRPORT. ANY DAY NOW THEY'LL RENAME
THE SÃO PAULO AIRPORT AFTER "GOLIAS" OR SOME OTHER
CLOWN. I HAVE PHOTOS OF IT AS GALEÃO PADRE ETERNO
W/ COMENTÁRIOS . . . FAIR WINDS. SEE YA SOON!
19:12 1/10/99 MARIO BANDEIRA

I have always been curious about why in the world the Rio
airport is named "Galeão". Though I asked a slew of *cariocas* that
question, Mário was the only one who actually researched it and
dug up the story behind the name.

The airport was named after a galleon, once billed as the
"greatest marvel the seas ever saw." The galleon, built in Rio
under a cloud of scandal and corruption during the Rio Revolt,
was launched in 1663 by then-Governor Salvador Correa de Sá
e Benavides, having been wondrously christened, PADRE ETERNO.

So now the Galeão Airport has been renamed *Tom Jobim*. Ac-
tually, the name is worse than that: it is *Maestro Antonio Carlos Jobim
International Airport*. This, in my opinion, will certainly make Tom
Jobim [one of the fathers of *bossa nova* music] roll over in his grave.

Given that my time is mine, and I gained an entire day, and a Saturday at that, I spend the rest of the day thinking about things that have nothing to do with the reality of that turbulent part of the world I am transiting. The topic of names comes up again.

What is it with our incurable tendency to impose the names of people—living or dead—on public places? And even more troublesome than that: why do we sometimes rename byways or places whose names bespeak their natural features—with the names of mere mortals?

For example, how did the road known as *Estrada dos Tropeiros*, which runs up the mountain between Paraty and Cunha, [a *tropeiro* was a driver who transported by mule goods up the mountain to sell to miners, then transported gold down the mountain to the port of Paraty, from where it was shipped to Portugal] how did that golden road earn the absolutely incongruous name of *Vice Prefeito Salvador whatever-his-name-was Street?*

Another example: the name of the street in Itapeví where we built our shipyard changed from *Estrada das Flores* [Flower Street] to *Rua Professor Waldemar Petená whatever-his-name-is.*

So many places have thus been blotted out of the public memory on behalf of the individual memories of a privileged few. Even in Paraty, the *Rua do Comércio*, the *Praça da Matriz*, the *Rua Fresca*, and the *Largo da Fonte* have given new names and street signs upon which mules and dogs urinate and cars roll—and no one will remember who those people were. In other places, for example, the *Estrada dos Trabalhadores (Street of the Workers)*, the *Cidade das Borboletas (City of the Butterflies)* there are plenty of examples of this dual disrespect. On the one hand, we erase the natural, authentic name of a place. Then, we usurp the name of a dead person—invariably without that person's consent.

Out on deck again, holding onto the handrail, I think aloud:

"My dear PARATII, in honor of the one who conceived your lines, if you do not make it home in one piece, I will rename you *Designer Roberto 'Cabo' de Mesquita Barros.*

Again, I tap the wood three times. I know how authentic Cabinho is—he'd kill me if I ever did such a thing.

11

AMUNDSEN SEA

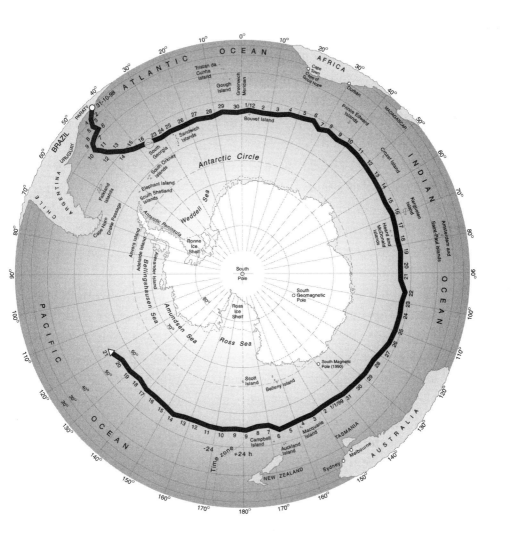

A series of depressions, or lows, are stacking up in the west. The current one, down to 980 millibars, is being followed by another one at 976, and yet another, even stronger and lower on the barometer, at 968 millibars. Gales and storms around here are named according to millibars; the lower the number, the more severe the storm. That's why they're called *depressions*—not because of their effect on one's psyche. They are meteorological and very real.

A low is a circular weather system. The direction the low is moving and its angle of approach to the boat determine the wind direction. As long as a low will hit us head-on, with northerly winds, it doesn't bother me much. Or rather, it doesn't drive me to despair. Neither am I terrified when lows come upon us from behind, with winds on the nose.

On the other hand, the calm between two big lows, when the wind stops but the seas remain heavy, is cruel torture and prolonged suffering. During those periods the waves, lacking an engine to drive them (that's the wind's job) churn up the sea surface into a confusing and disorienting mess. When there is no wind filling the sails, the boom bashes about helplessly with every roll of the boat, turning my life into a nightmare. These conditions pose the greatest risk to my mast.

The boom on the Aerorig system is heavy and rotates freely. The only time it becomes dangerous is in windless conditions, when it begins to slam back and forth. I rigged a preventer, kept at the ready for quick attachment to the boom during calms, to curb its erratic swinging. This line can also be used as an emergency mainsheet. But at the moment, nothing much is bothering me besides ominous weather forecasts.

My fingers suffer from the cold from time to time. All those lovely name-brand gloves made of GoreTex and other high-tech materials ending in "tex" are at best only good for building snowmen on deck—if the snow is dry. The poor quality of those famous brands makes me shiver. Friends I know who spend a lot of time mountain climbing, serious people who do heavy work in cold climes, warned me. Unfortunately, in the world of sporting goods it is hard to find reliable, heavy-duty materials.

I have had one pair of gloves of a type used by Japanese fishermen. They have none of that nonsense about "breathable" materials that become soaked in no time. I wore them whenever I went up on deck to handle wet lines, which requires finger-tip sensitivity for tying knots. The goal is to save time and fingers, which are always the first to freeze.

Back in Santos, we loaded and stowed a French-made thermal protective suit (TPS). It is light, with boots and gloves integrated into an intuitive single-unit design. Suits like this saved the lives of several sailors who lost their boats in frigid waters. Though I could wear it to stay warm in unbearably cold conditions, I keep it as a last resort, to put on just prior to abandoning the boat. So it remains stowed in a bright yellow bag in the stern locker. Every time I pass anywhere near that yellow bag I speak softly to it.

"Stay closed, my dear!"

Contrary to what some psychotherapists might think, I find talking with objects and myself a rather interesting and healthy exercise. I often launch into lengthy speeches on complex topics. Time passes more quickly that way. The struggle against the slow passage of time is the toughest battle of all.

Only three more weeks to go. Less than a month before I sight land again. I am eager to end my sojourn in the Pacific Ocean, to see mountains, to step on familiar rocks; but the clock is slowing to a crawl. My projections have me arriving in the Peninsula on February 3 or 4—if PARATII behaves and some freak low doesn't swallow us whole.

Unable to resist, after 10,000 miles plotted on the large chart, but always on its folded panes, I decide to unfold the chart for the first time. There is not enough space on the table, so I unfold it on the pilothouse floor.

Wow! Our plotted positions snaking around Antarctica now form more than a letter "C"! When I crossed 170°W, I had covered 255 degrees since leaving Grytviken. Only 105 degrees stand between us and the next waypoint, the Antarctic Peninsula, at 65°W. Just 30 degrees more and I will have completed the 360-degree circumnavigation as originally planned.

On the next pane of the chart I can see, at least on paper, the Antarctic Peninsula at one edge and Cape Horn at the other, on the southern tip of South America. From down here, Cape Horn looks cozy and familiar, so close to cities, villages, sheltered harbors, and good friends.

At the same time, I know that in any latitude and over any distance there is no such thing as risk-free sailing. Even the lazy bay in Jurumirim can put an end to a carelessly handled boat. Anybody can drown in a mere foot of water, and a small stone can sink a good boat.

Looking at the charts, I find comfort in seeing familiar land shapes. I take my eyes off the chart for a moment and stick my nose against the forward porthole to see where I am headed. YIKES! Now *there's* a familiar shape! It has been two weeks since I last saw an iceberg, but there goes one now, straight ahead! The radar, which is set to pick up anything twelve miles out, did not detect it. At six miles, the bugger pops onto the screen. It is very large, so I make a detour before we come too close.

January 16. We are at 58°S 140°W, with longitudes decreasing steadily. The Peninsula is only 75 degrees ahead and a little farther south. While working our way around yet another iceberg, with our bow facing slightly south of the white continent, another scare: an iceberg the size of a Volkswagen bug—damn! And, as if to end all prospects of joy and peace, a field of small icebergs pops up ahead. The radar did not see them, nor are they easy to spot with the naked eye. I'm glad Marina warned me on her last beeper message: "Be careful around the mouth of the Ross Sea." Once we pass the Ross Sea, we will have to cross the mouths of two other seas before reaching the Peninsula: the Amundsen and Bellingshausen Seas.

Russia's Thaddeus von Bellingshausen, with his two ships, VOSTOK and MIRNI, was officially the first to sight the seventh continent and the second to sail around it, 48 years after Cook's own circumnavigation. Bellingshausen's voyage, one of history's most unusual and noteworthy Antarctic circumnavigations, is perhaps also the least known. In addition to partially exploring South Georgia Island in 1819 and discovering the last three Sandwich Islands of the seven-island chain, Captain Bellingshausen also discovered, in the sea that today bears his name, two of the remotest and least visited islands on earth. The first was Peter I, which rivals Bouvetøya in its isolation, but wins outright in its inaccessibility. The second is Alexander, the largest island of the Antarctic Peninsula, located south of Marguerite Bay and eternally bonded to the continent by ice fields.

The first Antarctic wintering expedition, organized by Baron Adrien de Gerlache, took place exactly between these two remote islands. The BELGICA spent one year as a voluntary prisoner of the oceanic ice field. The expedition launched the career of Roald Amundsen, in my opinion the most brilliant polar explorer of all time.

Though competition for joining the expedition was fierce, Amundsen, a young Norwegian, was accepted based on the application letter he wrote to Baron de Gerlache, where his sincerity and objectivity shone through. That winter the crew, physically devastated by scurvy, and emotionally devastated by darkness, lost self-control and health.

Amundsen—whose name does not appear in Antarctica as frequently as his exploits would merit—met Dr. Frederick Cook aboard BELGICA, and they became friends. Years later, Dr. Cook claimed to have been the first person to reach the geographic North Pole. A controversy ensued over that claim—a bitter dispute between Cook and another explorer, Robert Peary. Ultimately, Cook was condemned, though the controversy has never truly been settled. Neither explorer was able to provide precise navigational evidence of having reached the exact location of the North Pole. Much later, as a result of this quarrel and in order to prevent repeating such errors, Amundsen adopted a procedure unprecedented in polar exploration. In striking contrast to British expeditions, Amundsen required that all of his men be qualified celestial navigators.

Amundsen's uniqueness as a historical figure goes beyond his naming of the remotest Antarctic seas. He reached the very pinnacle of success; no other explorer achieved so much. Yet, despite his success, his life was full of frustrations and difficulties, almost always financial, from which he was often saved at the last moment by friends or far-away sponsors. While greatly admired, he also made powerful enemies.

Once, he raised much-needed funds for his upcoming transpolar flight in the United States, and garnered the sponsorship of the National Geographic Society which had hired him to give a series of lectures, but he then managed to raise the ire of the press by paying a visit to his old friend Cook, who was sitting in a jail in Kansas City. The press despised Cook. The National Geographic Society reacted harshly to that visit, canceling Amundsen's lecture contract—a huge financial blow. According to Amundsen's personal code of ethics, loyalty to a friend who had been treated unfairly was more important than any geographic society, regardless of how necessary such societies might be and what the press might say.

It took almost 80 years for the National Geographic Society, Robert Peary's staunch defender in the dispute with Cook, to modify its position and acknowledge a historical snafu that Amundsen had detected from the outset. Neither Frederick Cook nor Robert Peary had the means to prove that they had reached 90° N latitude, and it is almost certain that neither man actually did.

Both the British and the Norwegians took photos to record the conquest of the South Pole. In the photos a tent can be seen—an aerodynamic tent designed by Cook himself. Of those old photos, my favorite is the one taken by Amundsen himself, poorly shot and out of focus. The British photo, of excellent quality, was taken with a time-lapse shutter. Captain Robert Falcon Scott, the leader of the expedition, is in the center of the photo.

During the final stretch of the 870 miles to reach the Pole, in a gesture of respect for his colleagues, and in honor of the Telemark skiers of Norway, the true pioneers of skiing, Amundsen asked his colleague Bjaaland to take the lead, ahead of the sleds. So the first to reach the South Pole was not a dog, as the British claim jokingly, but a ski champion from Morgedal, Telemark. A true sportsman. Therefore, even the toast, *Three cheers to the dogs!* is inaccurate, though it is sometimes still raised by the British at Antarctic gatherings.

The dogs did not arrive before the men did. It was the custom of the Norwegians always to send a leader ahead of the sleds, to keep everyone motivated. The sore-loser toast was first raised at a 1912 dinner sponsored by the Royal Geographic Society, in honor of Amundsen, shortly after the British defeat. Not only is the toast inaccurate; it is unfair. The British also used sled dogs to build their supply caches, and the fact is, they lacked the competence needed to finish the job.

Amundsen waited fifteen years to reveal, and only indirectly, the guilt he felt about Scott's death due to a lack of fuel for heaters in the final kilometers of the long trek back to the British camp. One of Scott's colleagues who survived, Apsley Cherry-Garrard, also felt guilty. Had Garrard simply disregarded Scott's confusing orders and poor leadership, and had he gone beyond the One Ton cache, as the initial plan had called for, he would have saved his hero and boss. Garrard only became aware of this fact seven months later, when the bodies of Scott, Wilson, and Bowers were found and dates in logs were compared.

While standing on the Pole, Amundsen was unaware that Scott was dragging his men to their deaths. Still, he considered leaving a supply of kerosene in the tent his team had erected to mark the spot, to be found and used if needed, by the British. On the other hand, Amundsen knew the British had departed much better-equipped than the Norwegians—with dogs, ponies, motorized sleds, and more men—so his thoughts turned to his own men, and he decided to take the vital fuel. Had he left the kerosene—a hypothetical question that cannot be answered—perhaps he could have saved Scott and his men.

Scott was a great writer. He did not write for himself but for the larger public, for the press, knowing that even if a tragedy were to occur, they would find his logs. Amundsen's writing, on the other hand, was devoid of emotion and dry. He did not describe his conquest as a feat that would glorify any particular race or nation of brave men, but rather, modestly, as the realization of a childhood dream. Well, it was actually the opposite of his childhood dream. On January 17, 1911, finally at the South Pole, the victor of one of the most extraordinary conquests in human history, Amundsen acknowledged that no man in the world was standing any farther from his true dream, which had always been the North Pole, on the opposite side of the globe. The truth is, in an era when nationalistic flag-plantings and heroics were more important than personal fulfillment, Amundsen had committed a crime of sorts; one of those crimes we can admire: he achieved his dream.

Down here at 58° latitude, utterly deprived of any light reading fare, I turn once again to old accounts of the heroic age of Antarctica's history. The bad thing is that I don't have any books on board with English names for Antarctica's geographical sites. The only book I have is Argentinean, which, because of Argentina's territorial claims and political pressures, either translates all geographical names, which should be a punishable crime, or worse, assigns new names. Nevertheless, it is always interesting to read the stories of how these places toward which I now travel got their names, however rough the seas outside and however tragic the story.

Halfway through January I have a miserable week. This is partly due to the books I have been reading, full of nationalist pride in heroism and bravery, the type of pride I abhor. It's a shame that most historians and chroniclers of great discoveries never themselves picked up a sextant to establish a position on the ocean. Nor did they ever experience on land the hardships of isolation or exposure to cold. The books I enjoy reading most, however dry they might be, are those written by people who actually lived what they write about and speak from their own experience.

Edward Wilson's log, with its watercolor illustrations, and Cherry-Garrard's book, *The Worst Journey in the World*, which I have on board—these are good examples of this kind of writing, even if they tried to defend Scott's blunders.

I try to moderate my personal considerations about British achievements, but the truth is that, in the history of polar conquests, the Norwegians were far more competent while using far less resources. No essay ever written by consultants, scholars, or anyone else provides more objective information about the planning and management of an expedition than does a straightforward study of the voyages of the FRAM and the GJØA. Not to mention the accounts of Nordic trade voyages to the Orient, or the more recent sagas of voyages to Greenland and America, circa 1000 AD. After years of work on the lines of PARATII II, a boat that will be even more prepared for long voyages, I have a much deeper appreciation now, while sailing, for the extent of the knowledge and good sense those sailors possessed.

Other men also possessed the same talents and applied those talents to building boats such as the *jangadas* made of local wood [the fishing boats native to the State of Ceará in Northeastern Brazil] the *vigilengas* [one-masted boats of the Amazon], and almost 200 other styles of boats built for plying the high seas and rivers. Those competent sailors have become inured to the disdain of modern navies. Often, upon sighting a *jangada* on the high seas, navy ships attempt to rescue the crudely built boat. To their shocked amazement, they discover a seafaring people that, after kindly refusing rescue, attempt to sell fresh fish to the ship's cook.

Admiral Antonio Alves Câmara, annoyed by Europe's disdain for Brazil's seafaring culture, and bothered by how little is known about Brazil's boat-building lore, drew from his vast knowledge of our coastlines to write one of the best books I own on the subject of Brazilian maritime culture: *A General Essay on Indigenous Naval Construction in Brazil.*

While I carry on these discussions with myself, using what few neurons are still working in my brain during a freezing gale, I glance up at the storm trysail, so boldly pulling PARATII along, when I heard a POW! I look around and see . . . the tiny imported ten-millimeter line. . . . Damn! The Marlow line, which cost me an arm and a leg, broke again. I grab the helm to prevent PARATII from broaching, and make ready to replace the line. Though lines of that brand are beautiful and multicolored, they are also the only lines that gave me any trouble underway (they came with the mast). Little by little I replace them with reliable lines.

Most of the running rigging on PARATII, even the anchor rode and heavy-duty lines (e.g. the lines for raising the centerboard), were manufactured by Cordoaria São Leopoldo in the state of Rio Grande do Sul, years and years ago. They are of excellent quality, and soft. In over ten years of use, they never let me down.

I love lines and ropes. Even when I'm driving a car I don't feel quite comfortable unless I have a set of lines and ropes in the trunk. I've spent many years traveling up and down Brazil's highways, constantly tying loads, or towing all kinds of vehicles. Along the way I learned from the driver of a horse-drawn wagon how to tie one of the handiest knots in the world. It's called the *carioca* knot, a knot used by Brazil's long-haul truckers. This knot, by the way, cannot be found in the *Ashley Book of Knots,* the bible of knot-tying. The knot is a huge success in circles of foreign sailors and mountain climbers. The *carioca* is a dynamic knot, with haul-down purchase points that allow the rope to be tightened at various places along its length. It's hard to explain, but it is efficient and easy to use.

Today's state-of-the-art sailboats usually replace chains, lines, and pieces of synthetic fiber with sophisticated hardware made of stainless steel or some other exotic material. These pieces of hardware are usually very expensive, heavy, and sophisticated beyond any practical usefulness.

But all it takes is one trip on a traditional *jangada* to appreciate the practical thinking and common sense applied with genius by those superb boat builders. On those "primitive vessels" one finds no nails, metal, or hardware, not even in the anchor, which is made of stitched wood and stone.

We had applied one of these marvelous solutions to PARATII's boom hoist point, back when the mast finally arrived in Santos. The boom's only hoist point, a piece that bears enormous responsibility, was poorly designed—set far away from the logical position for its purposes. To replace the piece of hardware would mean cutting, drilling, laminating, and reinforcing the whole boom. We decided instead to use a simple nylon and polyester woven belt, braced by a double round turn. It was a flawless solution. My friend Celsão, the king of parts, furnished the woven belt and buckle, which cost less than the price of two sandwiches and is still going strong, pulling PARATII eastward.

All those events seem so far away in time now, though they happened just a few months ago. Running around after endless tiny parts; welding the deck; Takako's numbered food boxes in a pile at the gate to Pier 26; checking the instruments; the programs I still didn't know how to use; the heat—all of that seems like a century ago now. Our nerves were so frayed back then, which was actually not our fault. Looking back on those days, I know that all of that could have been prevented.

Had the voyage begun one year earlier, as had been our original plan, it would now be over. Of course, I would not have leaped through time without paying the dues that come from traveling all these miles—as I sometimes now wished I could. But of one thing I am certain: despite everything, I would have departed well-prepared. Instead, I had to endure a one-year wait because of a delay in delivering a bought-and-paid-for part. It was tough to explain the delay to the bank that was sponsoring the voyage—much tougher than surfing those 60-foot waves over New Year's, south of Tasmania.

At that time, some friends assumed the delay meant that I had finally started thinking clearly and had given up on my deep-freeze endeavor. Others summed it up in a single finger-pointing word, chicken.

I had pressured Takako, Regina, and the girls at Nutrimental to package my meals in time for us to load PARATII and depart Brazil no later than November. But the mast, which was supposed to have been delivered in October, was not ready and would only be delivered eight months later. There was nothing we could do but wait, continue to harass the mast manufacturer, and wait some more.

Takako had very good reasons for the tantrum she eventually threw. The bank understood the dilemma and supported us above and beyond the call. If it had not done so, there would have been no boat, no mast, and no voyage. Other companies that supplied or supported the project showed the same solidarity: SAP installed the famous R-3 software; and Alcan and White Martins helped remodel the deck by welding aluminum brackets.

Those eight months of delay were converted into sheer work: testing and double-checking every detail of the boat and the voyage. By the time that "lost" year had passed, it had become a pivotal year for my plan's success.

Now, with 12,500 miles made good, almost 10,000 of which

have been sailed inside the Convergence, and after having sailed through over fifteen lows, it would be unfair to complain. We've had no torn sails, no problem that couldn't be fixed, the pharmacy hasn't been used at all, and all maintenance is up to date.

The only physical problem to speak of is my left ear. By habit, I always sleep in the pilot's bunk, stuffed into the sleeping bag with only my nose sticking out. I always face the instruments, which means, I always lay on my left ear. This is precautionary and self-serving. I can keep an eye on the instruments and the radar without having to shift my body, not even by the slightest movement. Over time I squashed my ear. Sometimes it hurts a little; then I quickly forget about it, just as I forget about so many other problems—plunging peacefully into the bliss of a few minutes of carefully-allocated forgetfulness.

12

THE BAY OF IEMANJÁ

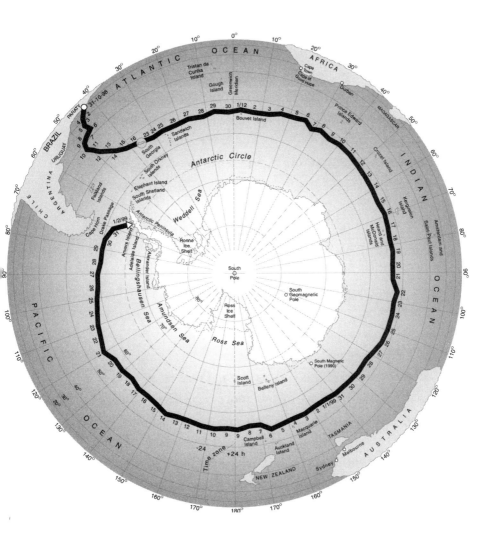

B zzzt, bzzzt. . . . Whoa! The little beeper is groaning. I jump from my bed, over the bunk's support tubes, and rip the little machine off of its tight Velcro spot on the bow porthole. Two messages. Let's see what's up!

27: MY LOVE, CONGRATULATIONS ON YESTERDAY'S PROGRESS—ADVANCING 6 DEGREES! GOOD NEWS. NEXT 36 HOURS WINDS 20 KNOTS FAVORABLE WAVES REDUCING TO 3 TO 5 METERS, BEWARE ANTARCTIC CONVERGENCE, SNOW FLURRIES—HEAVY ICE. KISSES FROM ME, IAIA AND THE BRUNETTE. 4:27 P.M. JAN. 14, 99

28: DEAR AMYR, GIULIANA, THELMA, AND I HAVE LOOKED AT THE ROUTE YOU HAVE COVERED SO FAR AND ARE VERY HAPPY. YOU ARE CLOSE . . . HOPE ALL IS WELL WITH YOU. MONDAY WILL ATTEMPT CONTACT BY SSB. FÁBIO TOZZI.

The onboard communications systems are working again— all of them. And this means news. The best news is that the good weather will hold up for two more days. In this world of constant surprises, even the slight prospect of stable weather can turn a couple of days into a carnival of happiness.

On Monday, as he had said he would, Fábio is on the radio with the other ham operators—Laslo, Lopes, and Ulysses. KOTIC is entering the Antarctic Peninsula, with the suitcase on board. We manage a triangulated conversation between two other boats and Brazil. Lots of news. Whereas I was enjoying relatively good weather—until the next lows come along—strong winds were thrashing the Drake Passage, 2,000 miles ahead of me. KOTIC had just traveled through it.

My French friend Hugo, who had wintered alone in Antarctica in the winter of 1990/1991 and lived on his boat for quite a while in Brazil, is hiding behind Cape Horn, before trying his third attempt at a crossing to Antarctica. As many French sailors based in Ushuaia, Hugo is transporting mountain climbers, who no doubt are waiting nervously. From New Zealand, behind and directly above my position, come news bulletins warning of bad weather. Warnings are broadcast every ten minutes (perfectly audible, which only make the news harder to bear) concerning Typhoon Dane, with winds up to 85 knots! "Thank God, that's a long way from here!" I think. Even with one ear flat as a pancake, zero-degree water temperatures, and a 20-knot breeze, it is comforting to be where I am.

January 20. I sail outside the area we had programmed for sending messages, which means no news from home either. Of course, I am busy looking at a strange iceberg six miles ahead. I have seen icebergs with some of the most absurd shapes imaginable, but this one seems one of the best. It is shaped, even at forty meters or more of height, exactly like, well, two breasts on a tray. The pinkish light of the sunset colors their peaks, making them look like the real thing. It reminds me of our prankster friend, Neka, not because of her breasts, mind you, but because of a gift she gave me once on my birthday—two plastic breasts with little feet that moved frenetically at the pull of a string. That gift was just like this berg's nippled breasts. There they are, dead ahead. Whoever designs icebergs has an absolutely limitless imagination. There is no longer enough light to take a photo, so I resort to drawing a rather interesting sketch in the log, all the more so, I'm sure, that for two whole months now I've seen no human form, breasted or otherwise.

At daybreak I see many more icebergs in a wide range of bizarre shapes: towers, castles, walls, animals. All have a common feature. Just as Neka's "breasts" rose out of a horizontal tray rimmed by a walled edge 30 feet tall, all the icebergs that follow are also served up on a similar tray, with walls like those of a cookie mold, well-formed and close to the waterline. One iceberg, whose tray edges are quite eroded, passes very near us. I do not adjust my course because I want to climb out on the boom and take a good look at this berg, to see what is inside its walls. What I see is a turquoise-colored lake large enough to shelter an entire fleet of sailboats. I do not have the nerve to draw in closer, but if I had brought along even one crewmember to help me, such as Fábio or Hermann, I would not have resisted the temptation to sail into that lake inside the iceberg. I call it the "geographic iceberg."

My boots are almost as eroded as these walls. I have others, but I like this particular pair and, at those latitudes, it goes beyond liking. The rubber trim is peeling off on all sides. My ongoing efforts to keep these fine boots serviceable yields yet another raw material out of which I could fashion insoles—this time I use cardboard I found in the workshop.

At one point, while I am seeking ways to make the boat go faster, with the barometer again scraping the bottom of the scale, the pager beeps, delivering a new and rather ambiguous message.

34: FORECAST ON 1/25/99 0:32: HIGH WAVES 35 FT NEAR LATITUDE 60°S, CURRENT PUSHING SOUTH, WAVES DECREASING IN 24 HOURS. WINDS 20 TO 40 KNOTS NORTH OF THE ANTARCTIC CONVERGENCE LINE. OVER 50 KNOTS.

The Bay of Iemanjá

WEATHER GOOD UNTIL ANTARCTICA PENINSULA IN 3 DAYS
WINDS STRONGER NEAR ANTARCTICA PENINSULA THEN
LIGHT WINDS. KISSES FROM YOUR FAVORITE MARINA.

What? How can the weather be good and winds light, at fifty knots!? It would have been better not to receive any forecast at all! I want the bliss of ignorance back. I try to pick up the weather-fax forecast issued by the Chilean Navy, but the notorious South American punctuality cuts off the transmission.

The next day the forecast plays out: a 40-knot wind is blasting across chaotic seas. Isn't that sweet? At least it is out of the west, I think, in feigned optimism.

I have a funny dream, and decide to jot it down. I finally arrive at the Antarctic Peninsula and, at one of the abandoned bases I discover a shipshape roomful of showers with hot water, new tiles, stainless steel faucets, fragrant shampoos. Though everything works, there is one caveat. The place has a dress code: suits and ties. I wake up trying to remember if I have a tie on board, or any other accoutrements of that order. Impossible!

It is raining buckets—at 60° latitude, of all crazy things! I keep wishing I could have at least made it through the shower before waking from my dream. I am badly in need of a bath, especially when I remember that today marks the 445th anniversary of the city of my birth, São Paulo, founded on January 25, 1554. To *Paulistanos* [natives of the city of São Paulo], this must be a holiday.

But this is just another day down here, albeit an eventful one. Not only do I cross below 60°S, but I also sail beyond the far edge of Nautical Chart No. 4009 and back onto the starting pane, the same one that contained positions from previous voyages scribbled in the right-hand margin. This first pane of the chart also bears the dotted line I sailed down to South Georgia Islands.

Coincidentally, on that Monday I also pass my last waypoint, No. 60-100, the imaginary intersection of latitude 60°S and longitude 100°W. From that point forward I am once again in the world of double-digit longitudes. On the same longitudinal line as PARATII but far to the north, is Mexico City. For some strange reason that has no real explanation, I feel as if I made it back to the Americas.

The windvane autopilot worked so many days and hours on end that one of its line-routing blocks explodes. I transfer the helm to the electronic autopilot and go down below to consult with the old junk box. I don't have any spare blocks, but I am able to surgically remove the needed part from an unused double block. Now, how will I graft the block back into place under a full gale while hanging off the stern? That is another story.

After two hours of hard labor I finish the operation. By some miracle I am still dry, so I enter PARATII celebrating yet another victory of man over machine. No waves hit me while I was engaged in that tricky operation. Only three waves engulfed the stern of the boat while I was out there, but they were so flamboyant and noisy in their approach that I had just enough time to scamper to my refuge high atop the stern arch, where the only danger I had to face was a wind generator that could have lopped off my ears.

Back down below, the same man who just conquered the machine outside gets whipped by the galley stove. While I am preparing to cook dinner in those extremely rough conditions, a package of instant mashed potatoes catapults from the countertop. As you might have guessed, the box is already opened. This sudden escape artist of a box slams into the wet wall, slides down to the wet floor, and turns into a spectacular puddle of highly nutritious greasy sludge.

The day would feel endless by now, if I had not received another message, this one from Villela, straight from the Weather Channel. Bleaker news than ever:

MESSAGE 13/2: VILLELA REPORTING: INTENSE LOW 968 MB
APPROACHING YOU FROM WNW. WIND VEERS FROM NW TO
SW STRONG. OVER 50 KNOTS. DECREASING. LOW MOVING
EASTWARD THROUGH DRAKE. TO AFT WINDS REMAIN
SSW . . . (INTERRUPTION . . .)

M14: REMAIN SSW HEADWINDS. YOU WILL PROBABLY
ENCOUNTER HEADWINDS WHEN YOU START HEADING TO
DORIAN. LATER FROM STERN AGAIN. PENINSULA BULLETINS
3/3 HOURS. PALMER ST. HF-ID. 8906.1 - 4067 MHS (45) 19:58
1/27/99. VILLELA.

The headwinds never arrive, but I am not wasting any time. Before the next low hits, I will drop further south as quickly as possible.

At 2:00 a.m., a sudden loud screeching sound—the autopilot screaming like a banshee. The motor, the autopilot motor! I return control of the boat to the windvane and go back down below. It is nothing serious. The motor of the electronic autopilot, after years and years of use, breathed its last. With my mountain climber's light strapped to my forehead, a few wrenches, and a new motor prepared in advance for easy installation, I switch the motors in minutes—and everything returns to normal. Nothing unusual is going on outside. My only concern is that I don't want to have any problems entering the Peninsula, so I am doing everything I can to make the boat run as if she were trying to win a race.

Messages keep coming through the pager:

M15/2: TODAY THEY LEARNED HOW TO SAY "PAPAGAIO"
[PARROT, IN PORTUGUESE]. THE BRUNETTE SAYS "PAPAGAIO"
AND THE BLONDE SAYS "PAPACAIO". WE LOVE YOU MUCH
MUCH MORE THAN YOU CAN IMAGINE. KISSES FROM THE 3
OF US: BLONDE, BRUNETTE, MARINA [48] 01:32 1/27/99.

VILELLA REPORTS: INTENSE LOW 968 MB APPROACHING YOU
FROM WNW. HEADWINDS NW-SW STRONG OVER 50 KNOTS.
DECREASING. LOW MOVING EASTWARD THROUGH DRAKE.
AFT WINDS REMAIN SSW [44] 19:49 1/27/99.

M17: IS THERE ANY WAY YOU CAN CALL BY INMARSAT
TELEPHONE? WILL IT TAKE LONG? KISSES.

M18: THERE'S NOT MUCH LEFT TO GO. WE LOVE YOU. KISSES
FROM LAURA, MONENA, MARINA.

Estimated arrival date: if the winds do not become headwinds,
February 2 or 3. A strong gale is forecast for the Peninsula on February 3 and 4. "My chances of dodging it are good," I write in the
log. By radio, I discover that Hugo was able to get across Drake Passage and is already on the Peninsula with his mountain climbers,
though he does not plan to stay very long. That's a pity. KOTIC, with
its hearty group of Brazilians on board, five in addition to Júlio and
Stickel, will drop off my suitcase full of surprises in Port Lockroy
and head for the Melchior Islands. But there is still a chance. I still
hope of getting there in time to hang out with those guys.

Saturday morning: I open the week's box of meals, box No.
14, and I stow trash bag No. 11 in the forecastle.

This evening during our radio QSO, Sérgio of the CASO SÉRIO comes on the frequency. He is swinging placidly at anchor in the clear green waters of Bracuí. He taught me a few words in Ukrainian, just in case I visit the Vernadsky base on the Argentine islands, the former site of Great Britain's Faraday base—an excellent Antarctic anchorage for sailboats. The opposite of their English predecessors, who were annoyed by visiting sailors, today's Ukrainians are warm and hospitable, according to reports from KOTIC.

The longitude of the Evangelista Islands lighthouse at the exit of the Magellan Straits falls behind us, as does New York in the northern hemisphere. I cross the longitude lines of the state of Acre in Brazil, and São Paulo, and Nossa Senhora da Glória, in the Amazon region. Although by latitudes these places are far away, it feels good to identify with them in terms of longitudinal proximity.

Sunday, Júlio radioes me the updated frequencies of the Chilean synoptic chart, and good advice: "There is a beauty of a low coming up from behind you, and if you don't arrive by February 3 you will have problems at the entrance to the Peninsula." The wind, which I now wished would be strong, drops to a miserable fifteen knots, leaving me no choice but to hoist the mainsail.

We pass more longitude lines: Cape Cod, Massachusetts and Punta Arenas, Chile. Only 260 more miles to the Melchior Islands. It has been a full three months since I left Jurumirim. I am having trouble falling asleep, but it is more important now than ever that I store up as much energy as possible for the final miles.

Monday begins in patchy fog, the effects of cold water and unusually warm air. When I entered the (– 4) time zone, instead of setting my watches to true local time, which would be two hours earlier than Brazil's daylight savings time, I decide to jump ahead, switching directly to Brazil time. Only one hundred miles separate me from land now. Though this is next to nothing, the distance from Paraty to Rio de Janeiro, it feels now like a million miles.

I suspect that KOTIC, chartered by passengers with tight schedules, will not hang around for this gale that is barreling down on me. I figure she will leave before we complete our rendezvous.

Acting on that, I go below and release the drive shaft—the brake fried long ago—and turn on PARATII's trusty engine.

"Sorry, folks. But I'm not going to drag my feet around here."

At 7:30 a.m. on Tuesday, February 2, a 15-knot nor'easter begins. I can make better time under sail and turn off the engine. At 8:10 I see a spot on the radar, 21.7 miles out. It can't be ice, but the fog is so thick I can't be sure of anything. At 9:15 Land ho! Land ho! Beautiful land!

It has been 72 days since I last saw land. Welcome, Brabant Island! I barely glimpse it, and it is gone. This is no longer fog, but heavy snow. This is wonderful! It's been so long.

The seas flatten, but not the winds. Six miles from the Melchior Islands—which are still invisible to me—we run into our first domestic iceberg, in calm waters. This berg is the real thing; it even has that distinctive smell. It smells of dry snow, of Antarctica—the smell of that place I love so much! It is February 2, *Iemanjá* Day [the day honoring the Goddess of the Sea]. What a gift!

And behold, on the bow appears an orange dot. A buoy? A navigational aid? What could it be? It turns out to be a gift from the Goddess of the Sea herself—a drifting orange fender. It is Norwegian. It must have been ripped off a ship. On my second pass I am able to grab it and bring it aboard.

At 7:27 a.m., on February 2, 1999, eight years to the date she departed from this same spot, PARATII drops her anchor once again in Dorian Bay, the bay of *Iemanjá*.

13

NINETY-TWO AND A HALF PERCENT OF MY DREAM

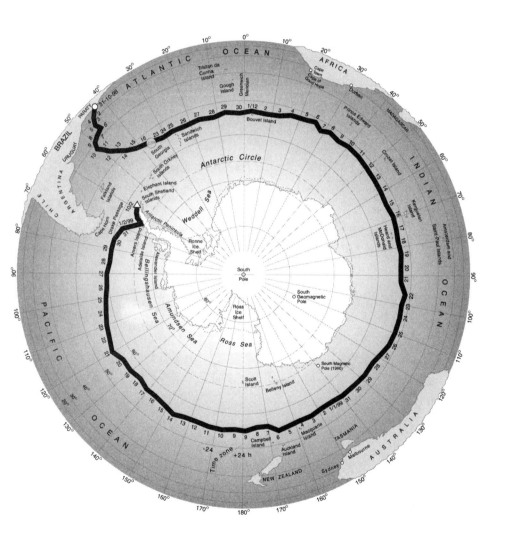

Flickers of light come through the glass door of the heater, and reflect on the control panel and the ceiling. Whenever strong gusts slam PARATII the flame vanishes, only to revive again a moment later. I am sitting on the old wooden bench in front of the heater with my sleeves rolled up, rubbing my hands on the heater's warm outer casing. It is cold. A nasty wind is blowing off Neumeyer Canal to the south. Inside, all is silence and comfort. The only sounds I hear are small bits of drifting ice scraping the hull on their way out into the bay. Very occasionally, gentoo penguins make some noise outside.

After two hours of running lines and chains between the boat and the rocks, and another two hours inside, cleaning the heater (it has been off for two months now), my fingers look like monster claws. Even after several washings with a super heavy-duty orange abrasive cleaner, my calluses and cuts are still full of coal and soot. I cannot describe the utter joy I feel, despite being soaked and salty, of being at anchor in Dorian Bay, of stepping on those old familiar rocks, seeking out holdings for the chains, of feeling PARATII solid as if on a foundation of rock. She is perfectly still, the grating of her mast finally silent, with not a hint of rolling.

After running a web of lines and chains among the rocks, the anchor, and the boat I am more exhausted than I would have been after a long day working the deck in nasty weather. The tide laughs at me as I wade, fully dressed, through the water, at times stooping and reaching down to secure lines to the best purchases the rocks afford me. Though I dunk myself several times, I am not complaining. It feels good to step on rocks for a change, as I firmly secure the red vessel that brought me here.

The second bow anchor has been set manually between rocks that are almost four feet underwater. When PARATII is finally securely moored, I tackle the heater. It was a good idea to take advantage of the remaining light to reset the lines. The barometer is in free fall, once again dropping off the scale. Because of Dorian Bay's topography, the gusts of a nor'easter tend to bifurcate as they arrive, roaring into the bay violently from both north and east.

Finally, back inside, in front of the fire that is working to heat up the boat's interior, I remove my boots and foul-weather gear. I put on dry clothes and make myself comfortable, with legs and raised arms outstretched. My feet are in pretty bad shape after a long time of work and sleep without ever removing my boots. This problem will have to wait until I take a bath—tomorrow. The howling wind and screaming penguins outside, their backs taking the brunt of the north wind, only add to the coziness of PARATII's interior.

I happen to know that two bottles of champagne are on board, both yet untouched, originally intended for Christmas and New Year, gifts from Marina and the girls at Nutrimental. As things turned out, the weather vagaries encountered at year end made me forget those bottles. I decided then, when that unforgettable low was dying out, that I would only open a bottle of champagne when there was truly something important to celebrate. Rather than a particular holiday or milestone, I would hold out for the simple act of setting foot on land—solid land. Right here, among these rocks I longed to reach. I wrap one of the bottles and two glasses in a jacket, tuck them into in a blue box, and go outside.

However, as I gaze out at the surrounding rocks, trying to choose one free of snow and flat enough to sit on, I remember that I have only covered 333 degrees of my planned 360-degree voyage. I still have 27 degrees to go before my circumnavigation is complete—7.5% of my trip still remains.

"What's the fun in celebrating 92.5% of a dream? It's an incomplete figure," I think. "Celebrate? No way, absolutely not. Only after we tie off the dotted line at the end of the journey, in South Georgia. End of discussion."

"But how about just a toast? Come on . . ."

The bottles go back below, to the bilge locker underneath the workshop. Instead, I dig up a fine Bordeaux, a more appropriate pairing with the cold outside—and with the pasta cooking in the galley. I serve the wine into one of the glasses, an authentic Murano blown glass brought all the way down here with tender care. I raise the glass to the photograph of Marina and the twins in a canoe resting ashore, and drink.

The wine is unbelievably good, a true survivor after so many miles of pounding. But honestly, if it had been vinegar it would still have been the finest wine I ever tasted. To be in Dorian Bay now, after 333 degrees of endless bronco-riding across the seas, I feel so happy. If I had continued straight for South Georgia Island, between latitudes 57° and 60°, the sea would have gone on forever—an endless sea. But on January 29, I crossed latitude 60° and once again entered into chart No. 3200, southward toward the Peninsula that brought me to that place. Though there are many Antarctic paradises, at this moment I only have eyes for that precious bay.

My decision to make landfall here is not tied merely to the fact that I missed the place that had been my home for a year of my life. Anyone lucky enough to arrive into that bay would fall in love with it, regardless of his or her feelings about the cold or sea.

Spending a full year there would only deepen that love because of memories left behind, and small buried treasures waiting to be found. Sure, a first visit might be attributable to chance. But there is no luck involved in my decision to return. No, I have chosen to anchor right here because of a specific wish: to satisfy my nostalgia for the rocks of Dorian Bay.

Now, I am lucky to get into the bay in one piece. It would have been easy to fail, considering the many icebergs, lows, and crises we encountered. But from the moment I left that rotting wooden pier in Grytviken, I was determined not to stop until I reached those beloved rocks. For seventy-two days, whenever I looked at PARATII's anchor, I knew precisely where I wanted to drop it: 64°48.97'S and 63°29.95'W. It might seem such a meaningless target, but I wasn't for me. And I reached it. I traveled 12,240 nautical miles to reach the spot where I dropped anchor.

My watch, an infallible G-Shock, finally comes off my right wrist. Time has stopped. The second glass of wine makes me dizzy, so I stop drinking. There is no reason to get drunk and confuse my judgment. No, I want just the opposite, to enjoy what little clarity of mind I still possess. I take down the pilothouse berth, reassemble it below, and roll into a fresh, dry sleeping bag. In a fit of giddy laughter, I turn off the world—with no scheduled time to turn it on again.

My first night of sleep is restless. Not only the wind doesn't let up, but I have forgotten how to sleep for hours on end.

In the morning, while I warm my hands around my first cup of coffee (I can actually set the coffee cup down without it flying off the table!), I hear a bang followed by a loud cracking sound of hollow rock coming from astern, on the south side of the bay. One of PARATII's lines went slack and she begins to move. This makes no sense at all. I set down my coffee, go outside, and tug on the line. It is loose! Actually, it is still attached to the rock by chains and shackles—but this is not the same rock! The original rock to which I attached the line was about six feet wide and twelve feet high, thicker than one of Easter Island's *moai* stone statues. But it broke in half, right down the middle.

"My God! I broke a piece of the bay!"

I immediately jump into the orange dinghy that was lazing in the water and row over to the rock. It doesn't seem real that a rock of that size could break in half, cut horizontally as if with a saw. But nothing is impossible around here. Luckily the chain, still wrapped around the portion of rock that fell, was not crushed; I am able to salvage it with no problem.

During that episode, PARATII's stern remains tied by a second line that was attached in an interesting way. While preparing for the voyage I knew that if I did not make it into Dorian Bay and was forced to seek improvised shelter for PARATII in an unknown bay, my toughest job would be attaching lines to rocks. The people at Bosch do Brasil helped me put together a set of drills and bits that would allow me to sink pad eyes on any type of rock surface, smooth or rough. We tested the procedures in Paraty; it worked perfectly. One of the drills was battery-powered and the backup drill ran on a mini-generator. If all else failed, I would use a manual rock-drilling system I had used in Paraty.

As it turns out, when I arrive in Dorian Bay, though the entire system, including the generator, would have been lighter than my basket of shackles and chains, I choose instead (out of respect for the bay or for the rocks themselves, I'm not sure which) not to drill holes or leave any permanent marks. If I'd had permanent stainless steel pad eyes, or even galvanized ones like I've used in Paraty, perhaps. But my pad eyes are for temporary use, made of carbon steel, and they would have left rust marks on the rocks for all eternity.

So, instead, I use a Swedish system, so simple a child could almost do it, and infallible when tying boats to fissured rocks in the Baltic Sea. The solution involves setting into a fissure a small, asymmetric T-shaped fastener that has an eyelet on one of its ends. Fissures are plentiful, so I use these little doodads to tie up PARATII with a strong backup line. In fact, the number of fissures in the rocks of Dorian Bay might explain why such a large rock (which, by the way, did not have fissures) could break in half so easily. Obviously, the rocks that fill this bay are under enormous stress (there are many loose rocks, neatly cut in two, to prove the point). Water and ice infiltrate the rocks year after year, expanding the fissures and turning the shoreline into a living mosaic of new rocks born every time old rocks break.

Anyway, I rework the attachment for the main line in seconds, while in a loud voice thanking my friend Luís Oswaldo, who months earlier provided me with those little T-fasteners.

Breaking rocks was a skill I learned over many years in Paraty, where we had used rock to build walls, columns, and even a ramp to haul ROSA (my beloved log-hewn canoe), and many other, much larger boats. By always using local materials, we were doing things the way they had done them in the old days, and to this day the method for breaking rocks hasn't changed. A steel bar is forged in fire with a leather and mud bellows, its sharp ends hardened under fine sheets of water. Sometimes we made low-grade gunpowder using saltpeter, sulfur, and coal straight from the fire, a primitive craft that still works. I guess I have become accustomed to the idea that gigantic rocks lying across a path can be removed in a matter of hours. Feijão, Lindomar, and old "seu Zé" are Paraty-born experts in this field.

I'll never forget an observation Joaquim made about rocks, a long time ago. We were walking with machetes and scythes in hand, up Caboclo Hill, behind the city. We were seeking a route through which an old Lanz, a tractor with a 40-hp, 2-stroke engine dating from the war era, could reach our fields of beans. There was an old path, now overgrown by gigantic trees. A huge *tarumã*, a beautiful and fast-growing white wood tree, was lying across the path, its roots wrapped around an enormous black boulder. Impatient, tired, scratched by a thousand thorns and with a bloodthirsty leech on my leg, I didn't give it a second thought.

"The rock goes!" I said to Joaquim. "The tree stays."

He knew how much I love trees. He responded, "I don't know about that. That's not the best idea at all. The *tarumã* trees grow like weeds; we can plant a bunch of them. But have you ever considered how long it took to grow that rock?"

In the end neither the rock nor the tree were removed. I borrowed one of Joaquim's cigarettes and burned the leech off my leg, and then we calmly came up with a plan that would allow us to bypass both. Joaquim was right: rocks take a long time to grow. We'd best leave them alone.

The angular and tortured rocks of Dorian Bay in some ways remind me of the calm, dark rocks of Jurumirim. In both cases, these rocks form a ring around their respective bays, to me the most important bays in the world. Both have slightly muddy bottoms. The mud that still clings stubbornly to the anchor chain when I drop the anchor in Dorian Bay is mud from my home bay in Jurumirim. During our stopover in Grytviken, PARATII did not anchor, but remained tied to the old whaling dock.

Later, as I watch PARATII from the summit of a far-off rocky hill, I imagine our next anchorage. If we make no further stops on the Peninsula, the next stop could very well be Jurumirim. At rest my boat, high up on a hill with snow falling heavily, looks magnificent. It has been snowing and raining all day. Before long the weather is sure to clear up and reveal the shape of Anvers Island and its famous peaks. Most delightful of all, PARATII is all by herself, the lone occupant of the bay.

During the descent from the Pacific Ocean to the Peninsula I maintained daily communication with KOTIC and the gang on board. Wisely, when they reached the Melchior Islands they decided to head on up to Cape Horn before a low bearing down on them could catch them. Júlio, by radio, told me about more than half a dozen sailors supposedly in Antarctica. I know some of them. Hugo, of the sailboat IF, lost a lot of time in his four attempts to cross Drake Passage, and the chartering mountain climbers did not want to dawdle down here. There was one singlehander, a very young guy from New Zealand, still searching for a place to hole up for the winter. Jerôme Poncet too, left the Peninsula. I ran into Jerôme back at Grytviken, where he presented me with a full bottle of single-malt Scotch as a gift. The red steel sailboat belonging to the strange Dutch guy who almost crunched my boat in Grytviken, has also already departed. So the best surprise of all when I arrive in Dorian is to find the bay empty of all masts, empty of all people. Not that I am being antisocial. I just want to spend a few days in peace, getting reacquainted with the bay. After that, I'll be up for anything, even Carnival.

This return to a peaceful Dorian Bay includes some providential surprises, such as finding an old English cabin, just a shelter now, that in the past served as an outpost for operations of the British Antarctic Survey (BAS). But its color has changed. It had once been painted a joyful sunset pink; now, it is a rather sad color, institutional green. The no longer pink cabin contains a rare collection of polar books, available for reading *in situ*. Rather than lending them out only to have the books disappear, each new expedition or visitor brings new volumes to add to the collection.

My first venture in the little orange dinghy is to Port Lockroy, three miles south, where I run into two friendly British guys who are finishing a project restoring and cleaning up the old base. I also pick up my suitcase full of surprises from Brazil. Dave, the older of the two, gives me a gift: a plastic bag filled with grapefruit, oranges, two apples, cabbage, and some potatoes, the first fresh food items I have eaten in two and a half months. He cannot explain the dreadful color of the cabin on Dorian Bay, but I don't press him too hard, either. I am concerned about PARATII being all alone with the heater on, so I return quickly to my bay.

The opening of the suitcase is such a special event that it delays my onboard work and maintenance schedule by two full days. Two beautiful days during which I do absolutely nothing useful. Letters from friends, newspapers, magazines, photos of the girls (my goodness, how they have grown since October!), a cassette recording of the voices of my little "blonde" and my little "brunette." I hang up the photos with Velcro strips Tigrão put into the suitcase. That ragtag black plastic suitcase, held together with duct tape, turns out to be a treasure trove. Saul sent the new telephone with a friendly message from the folks at Iridium in Rio. Within seconds I am dialing home. A city cell phone user, taking such technology for granted, simply cannot comprehend how revolutionary this phone is to the sailing world.

Today is the twins' first day of school. I can picture them heading off in their little uniforms. While talking with Marina I hear the brunette saying, "*babai, balélia, vóca, bexe, pimpim* . . ." [n.t.: baby Portuguese words for "daddy, whale, seal, fish, penguin . . ."].

With so many high-priority tasks to be completed during my stopover in Dorian Bay—I have already done some general housecleaning, so PARATII is in pretty good shape—the next important one is taking a bath. I really have no idea what I look like at this point. During January, I managed to break all previous personal records for time spent away from soap and fresh water. I crave a hot bath more than anything in the world. Though I knew my feet were in bad shape, I didn't know how bad. While showering, I notice that at least one foot is a good candidate for research at the Butantã Institute, alongside the amputated limbs of fatal snake-bite victims, preserved in a jar filled with formaldehyde. I am fascinated to see the state of my toes and sole. Effortlessly, I peel off whole sheets of dead skin. That's what ten weeks straight wearing boots day and night will do to your feet.

After the magnificent bath, both shower and tub, I tackle the laundry. I take four boxes and two buckets of salty clothing to the rock-rimmed pools on the south side of the bay. First the clothes are desalinated, and then washed in running water. Initially, I use gloves and an oar from Paraty to stir the clothes in a crude human-propelled washing machine. As I warm up with the exercise, I roll up my sleeves and attack the job bare-handed.

Those few days in Dorian Bay may feel like the best days of my life, but I dare not completely relax. The weather improves, though the barometer is still extremely low. I get more rest than I've had in years, and I have the pleasure of two visits. The first is by two mountain climbing guides from New Zealand. They were dropped off by a ship to attempt to scale Mt. Français, the highest peak in the region, on Anvers Island, directly on PARATII's nose. They depart through the Neumayer Channel in a small overloaded dinghy, which they plan to bury in the snow on the other side. When they leave they are still having problems with their kerosene stoves and radios. Unfortunately, I never hear any further news about them.

The second visitor is Suzana, a tall, blond Brazilian woman, who pilots one of CALEDONIAN STAR's inflatable dinghies. I am down in the engine room performing the unpleasant task of

Secure in Dorian Bay, though it can be exposed to catabatic winds.

checking filters and lubricants and almost fall backwards when I hear shouts from outside. Party time, again! I visit the ship, take a bath in the ship's sauna, and try what few words I know in Swedish—mostly curses—on the crew.

Many of the dinghy operators on these small ships, who also serve as guides, are female. These women are more competent than most male sailors I know, and are charged with the task of getting people on and out of the planet's most inhospitable shorelines, often in dangerous wind and storms.

The LINDBLAD EXPLORER, and its successor, WORLD DISCOVERER, are pioneer cruise ships. Using small, often Russian-made ships, these cruises visit remote areas known for their virgin beauty. These places, chosen because of their rare natural features, do not have ports, so the cruise ships rely on the black rubber dinghies for loading and unloading. The cruises themselves are flexible and informal. Instead of gala dinners, swimming pools, and other such nonsense, researchers and explorers are invited along to give lectures in the evenings and participate in outings during the day.

In my quick visit aboard CALEDONIAN STAR I learn that the ship makes only two stops in Brazil. One is at a beach in the state of Bahia, called Itacolomis. The other stop, and this is an unbelievable coincidence, is precisely in Jurumirim. I almost fall over backwards. Passengers did not disembark in nearby Angra do Reis, or even in Paraty (nearer still), but precisely at Jurumirim. The crew knows that little bay like the back of their hands. "I guess so," I think. "You'd have to, to get a large boat like this in that little fjord . . ."

Just as quickly as she arrived, in less than two hours CALEDONIAN is gone. I return to the peace of Dorian Bay. It is a magnificent day. For the first time in five days, I am able see Mt. Français. No sign of the mountain climbing guides. We had agreed to get in contact on a particular frequency, but all I hear is silence. I spend the day outside collecting freshwater from springs, and walking. In the afternoon I take advantage of the total calm to replace the mainsail. A seam has begun to unravel high up the mainsail leech. It is an important seam that chafed against a lazy jack and will require new stitching. Better to replace it with a spare than to rely on a makeshift repair.

I calculate how much water I need for the remainder of the voyage, which gives me a reason not to sleep and then I start thinking about the 27 degrees still needed to complete the circumnavigation. That is why I am restless. Despite my love for this paradise, I know I cannot stay around here any longer.

Tuesday, February 9. I am clean and in good shape. The boat is heated and all systems have been checked. The new mainsail is ready; it is time to leave Dorian Bay, I am not staying here another minute. I gather all the hardware I used in mooring the boat to rocks and anchors, cast off, and slip out of the bay. The centerboard, which is lowered, bangs the bottom twice, hard, as we snake through rocks guarding the narrow mouth of the bay: BOING! BOING!

"Farewell, Dorian Bay! See you next time!" I yell. It is 7:50 a.m.

The pressure returns within the scale, rising. The Brazilian Navy's forecast called for a big new low that is expected to hit the Peninsula within two days. I leave without knowing quite where to stop next. I will make my decisions based on where I am and how exhausted, stopping either at Deception Crater or heading straight for the Brazilian station, 210 miles to the northeast. If the bad weather catches up with me before making landfall, I will run for the high seas, where everything is easier when you're single-handed. I put on my blue knit cap and sit on deck under the sun. I hold the helm. Though at first this kind of coastal sailing should be relaxing, it will soon become stressful because sleep is out of the question for the next thirty-six hours. I will be too busy, dodging icebergs and islands.

After leaving the Neumayer Channel, I enter the Gerlache Strait and find myself surrounded by the blowing spouts of humpback whales. This scenic crossing where a small channel runs into a large on is a traditional gathering place for the whales.

A short, triangular iceberg appears to the north. An iceberg on the move . . . with a mast . . .

"It's a sailboat, it's a sailboat!" I yell, grabbing my binoculars. "Finally, another sailboat!"

Before I can make the first move, the boat changes its heading and comes toward us. At 2:27 p.m. with just a few feet separating us, we pass each other, going in opposite directions. The boat is full of people. I shout in French, the *lingua franca* in this region. A funny-looking guy is at the helm with a camera hanging around his neck. He answers my call.

"Ciao, Amyr!"

It is Giorgio, an Italian who knows Paraty well and lives in Ushuaia on a sailboat called SAUDADE. Giorgio comes about and for ten minutes we shout at each other in Portuguese, to the befuddlement of the rest of the ship's company, who don't not recognize this strange language.

By pure coincidence, that same evening at 10:06 p.m., while on the radio with Brazil, my friend Pedrão comes on the air. Pedrão is a professional sailor who constantly delivers sailboats back and forth across the Atlantic. He is on his way to Barbados and knows Giorgio and SAUDADE very well. Within seconds he gives me all of the boat's specifications. It is a 47-foot French-made Amel, built of fiberglass and ugly as hell, but according to its builders, bullet-proof. "That's the kind of boat you want in Brazil," I think.

The winds are out of the northwest and extremely light. The motor is rumbling along, and the sails are full. I am rummaging around for a comfortable place to nap before the low rolls in, still wearing the blue knit cap from the YELCHO. This cap survived the year-end storm; I like wearing it in extreme circumstances, in the desperate absence of good weather. An officer of the Chilean ship, YELCHO, presented the cap to me as a gift, many years ago. The original YELCHO, whose bow is planted in Port Williams in the Beagle Channel, was a legendary ship. On August 30, 1916, under the command of its pilot, Pardo, YELCHO sailed off on a major undertaking—Ernest Shackleton's fifth, and finally successful, attempt to reach Elephant Island and rescue the twenty-two men he had left stranded there years earlier.

*   *   *

Twenty-four hours after leaving Dorian Bay the entrance to Deception Crater is on my port side, with its "Neptune Bellows" apparently catching their breath. The island's narrow entrance is famous for strong local winds that make life difficult for boats passing through. Thus, the name. Fortunately, the wind is not blowing violently at the moment. Twenty-four months ago I passed through here with Fábio, aboard a Russian ship, when another boat, a Chilean tugboat under full throttle, struck a sharp rock that tore the hull below the waterline, contaminating the boat's tanks. Even in places with frequent traffic, such as this passage, there are still many uncharted hazards on the Peninsula; in some spots, whole regions are uncharted. The wind is light so I decide not to enter, but head directly for the Brazilian station. I can't wait to practice my Portuguese and my good manners again.

The Brazilian station is located on King George Island, eighty miles beyond Deception Island, or ten hours sailing at eight knots. The scenery here is completely different from the southern part of the Peninsula. There are open spaces; icebergs are much larger. I even see some tabular ones. Despite being open and spacious, the area is not very welcoming, offering few decent shelters for small vessels such as PARATII. Deception Island, the last good shelter for small boats exiting the Peninsula, soon falls away astern. A member of the South Shetland Islands, Deception gets the least amount of snow and is the only island with frequent volcanic activity. One of the half-moon bays inside the crater, Telephone Bay, has waters warm enough for swimming. On the other side of the same bay is Pendulum Cove, a reasonable harbor for shoal-draft vessels. The only unsafe anchorage during a gale is out in the deep water of any of Deception Island's half-moon bays.

If my destination had been Cape Horn, this would have been a good place to make one last stopover before leaving the Peninsula. Cape Horn is only 450 miles to the north-northwest, and the

Falkland Islands are 630 miles north of here. But my objective is South Georgia Island, much further east. Regardless, by pressing on I will end up at the mouth of Admiralty Bay, where the Brazilians are. I think it wisest to take advantage of the good weather and swallow up those eighty miles.

Following the northern edge of Bransfield Strait, which separates Deception and the Shetland Islands from the Peninsula, I can hardly see the other side, the continent itself. The snowcaps atop the Antarctic mountains, reddening at end of the day, will be my last visual contact with the Antarctic continent.

When we reach Livingstone Island the wind shifts blissfully to the south. PARATII picks up speed. Almost thirty hours without sleep . . . and another half-dozen to go. I drink one cup of coffee after another. Sailing like this, in monotony and silence, adds a nervous edge to it. My only fear is that I might become drowsy. If my eyelids become heavy, the plan is to ditch the visit to the Brazilian station and run straight out into the open seas. Iceberg sightings are rare; at the moment I can see just one, a large tabular berg, off to starboard.

I am minding my own business on deck, the blue cap yanked down over my ears and trying to keep my hands warm on my belly, when I almost have a heart attack. A large black dorsal fin rises just ahead of the bow, touches the side of the hull, and sends an impressive spoutful of water all over the boat. What a mischievous humpback! It touches us, sneezes and vanishes. Talk about startled! The deck is still all wet though the whale itself is already long gone.

"How can anyone sleep under these conditions?" I yell.

At precisely 8:05 p.m., Brazil time, dinner time, with the barometer high and the weather clear, I drop anchor for the second time of the voyage. I lower the mainsail and furl the jib, euphoric that I won this race. I beat the low. "Wow! At last, a civilized place to catch up on lost sleep," I think. I know that the runner-up in the race, the low, is right on our tail and barreling down on our position.

While I use my foot to test the tension on the anchor chain, to make certain the anchor is holding, it occurs to me that the next place I will drop anchor, if all goes well, will be in Brazil. On South Georgia Island I won't anchor but tie up at the pier. Besides, I will only be there long enough to let the bad weather roll through. The front must be getting close. It will probably pound us with the force of a samba marching band. The fact this is Carnival Week back home has gone unnoticed. If I could imagine, for one second, the parade we are about to watch, I would turn myself into an albatross and fly off the map.

14

RETURN TO THE OPEN SEA

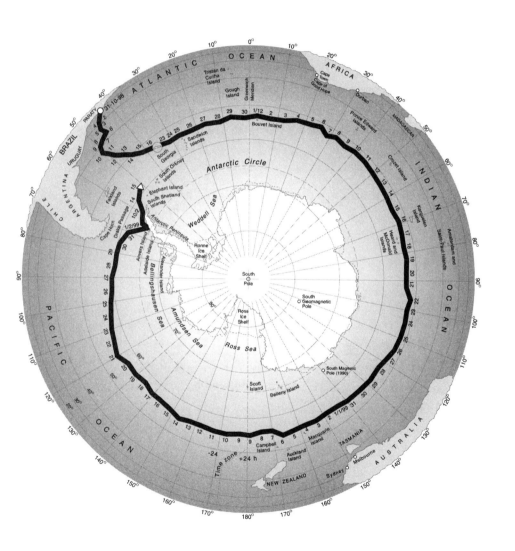

Brazilians are accused of having short memory spans, of being disorganized and lacking punctuality. They are incapable of saying no, and hate to think about the future. But for these attributes, a trait shines that has become our trademark in this age of egocentrism and competitiveness, namely, our hospitality. The less Brazilians run after material goods and urban lifestyles, the more hospitable they are; farther into the interior of the country, it is rare to find people who are cold and indifferent toward others.

There's nothing that can compare to finding yourself in the middle of a group of Brazilians working far from home. I have visited American, Russian, and Scandinavian stations; I stayed in the homes of relatives and friends around the world. What a difference here, in Antarctica no less, where I am now enjoying the incomparable warmth of a group of Brazilians.

Of course, I did everything wrong. Protocol required me to first contact the station command post by radio, requesting authorization to make the visit, and only then to set a schedule. But, because I wasn't sure I would anchor here in the first place, when I finally do, I just decide to arrive unannounced at the station.

Within five minutes I feel completely at home. I take a hot bath, my third of the year. I am given a towel, shampoo, and deodorant—and a burst of new life. Dinner is served: rice and beans, peppered chicken, and endless conversation. There has never been a more perfect example of Brazilian hospitality than what I find at the Comandante Ferraz Antarctic Station.

*   *   *

Commanders Aquino and Iran insist that I stay at the station and sleep in one of the vacant bunks, but it would not be prudent to leave PARATII alone in a bay as exposed as this one, with its propensity for gales and williwaws. I thank them and return to my aluminum home, hitching a ride from Helena, a mountain climber, and sub-commander Wagner, a.k.a. Sub. Darkness falls. I fall asleep only after spending a full hour monitoring PARATII's position relative to the station's lights, making certain the anchor is not dragging.

The next morning I decline the invitation to breakfast. Actually, I have lost all track of time. I also lose my good mood when I read the barograph. Since midnight the device has been dropping steadily, punctuated by small downward spikes. While I was sleeping the skies became overcast. From deep inside the bay, blocks of ice drift outward and gather to the north and south of PARATII, where they settle atop two submerged rock formations that provide a modicum of protection to the boat; none of the chunks threatens to snag the chain and drag me away.

I accept the invitation to lunch. The cozy friendliness of the cafeteria seals us off from the cold outside, and the noise. The high pitch of lively conversation makes it impossible to hear the howling wind gusts. From time to time I can see PARATII's mast holding itself in line with a *nunatak*, a rock jutting through the glacier across the bay.

After dessert, I pitch in with the housecleaning in the video room, lifting chairs so Commander Aquino's broom can reach the spaces underneath them. Suddenly, Viana, who has been standing at the window watching the wind, shouts an alarm.

"PARATII broke loose! PARATII broke loose! She's headed toward Arctowski!"

I race out, skating across the wood floor in my socks—no

shoes are allowed inside the station. The commander comes along behind me, trying to calm me down.

There's more to it than just simply stepping outdoors. First you have to go through the "incubator," a super-heated room (a modified shipping container, really) where cold-weather gear is stored alongside orange survival suits, gloves, boots, and anything else that was removed on entry, left there to dry. The place is a human oven.

An alert is issued to the boathouse. "Prepare Boat Number One for rescue!" Viana, Dos Anjos, Sub, and I will be the crew.

By the time we step out of the oven-like area, we are perspiring, and the wind is fierce and blowing straight onto the beach. Bits of ice flotsam churn in the waves. It doesn't seem logical that the wind could be blowing PARATII so far away from us, while simultaneously blowing straight toward us here at the beach. I am not wearing a survival suit, but my everyday sailing clothes, ridiculously inadequate in such a situation.

As we try to launch Boat Number One, wind gusts blast spray and foam across the surface of the water. Every time we roll the trailer backwards into the water, waves launch both boat and trailer back onto the beach. The boat is quickly swamped with water and ice.

Wagner wades into the waves up to his neck and grabs the transom while we try to keep the boat from dashing against the rocks. Dos Anjos, strong and calm, does his best to stand in the aft part of the boat, now full of water, and he yanks on the starting cord. By the looks of it, his right arm alone packs fifty horsepower. On, two, three . . . ten, eleven yanks. The motor is flooded. Waves crash against the transom. I simply cannot believe what is happening. I begin to shout.

"This thing is not going to work! The motor is loose!"

Meanwhile, PARATII is drifting farther and farther away—sort of sailing away, actually. The outboard dies again. Wagner and Viana then hold the motor while I give the cord a pull, allowing Dos Anjos to catch his breath. I continue to shout. At that point, Dos Anjos, calm and thoroughly soaked, places a vise grip hold on my arm. Turning his head sideways to offset the howling wind, he says in a serious and firm tone, "Calm down. This is going to work and we will get your boat."

The motor sputters, but starts. The three of us belly-jump like seals into the boat while Dos Anjos takes the tiller. The sea is a choppy, foamy mess as the overloaded little boat slams against the waves. It looks as if the outboard motor will bounce off its bracket at any moment. The minutes go on forever. PARATII is sailing away under the power of her bare mast, heeling, and dragging the chains and anchor that still hang from her bow.

As we get closer, the sight grows even worse. My dear PARATII, my home, still some hundred feet away, is running under her own power for the high seas. While we angle in for our approach, seeking the most promising spot for our assault onto her decks, the motor dies again. Sub uses the radio, soaked but still working, to order Boat Number Two to be launched immediately, to rescue Boat Number One.

No, this can't be happening. What a nightmare. The outboard is flooded again. First Viana, then Sub, then I—ten, eleven, twelve pulls on the cord . . .

I keep muttering, "This isn't happening. This isn't happening." Until finally someone—I don't see who it is, because I am out of breath, shaking, and exhausted with the effort—manages to get the damn thing to start.

In those few seconds the wind again pushes us far away from PARATII. Making slow progress, freezing, and drenched, we finally reach her. This time it works.

I leap onto the stern platform, shouting that I can handle

things by myself, but Sub doesn't wait and jumps aboard too, so quickly that I don't even know exactly where he comes aboard. Boat Number Two, which was already leaving the station to rescue Boat Number One, turns back; and Boat Number One heads back to Ferraz Station. I am soaked to the bone. If it had not been for the calm of those individuals and their energy, I would have lost everything. I am grateful.

Calmly, I begin to straighten out the deck, making preparations to haul in the rode and anchor. I encourage Wagner to go below to escape the wind while I am trying to figure out what sin I committed to merit this sort of punishment.

The two men still in Boat Number One, now a long way off, disappear from sight amidst the waves and blowing spray. If anything were to happen to them it would be my fault. Seconds later, Sub steps out from the companionway and calmly notifies me, "There's a fire below decks."

"What?"

"Something's on fire in the saloon."

I step inside into a dark, smoke-filled hole. All I can see in the center of the smoke are flames around the heater. The damn heater! Its outer casing is ringed by fire. What a mistake not to have turned it off before heading ashore. The wooden central column in the salon is ablaze. I cut off the fuel feed and remember a red-letter warning I read in the manual: *flooded burner*. It has finally happened.

Damn heater! I should have brought my old Danish Reflex heater, which would not have flooded the burner so easily. It is too late. *Mea culpa, mea culpa!*

"Stop, you cursed machine, stop!" I yell as I try to cover the heater with wet towels and floor mats. It takes a while, but it finally blows out. The fires on the heater and on the column are out, but it only makes the smoke thicker. Before I can gather my first thought, coughing because of the smoke, I hear Sub say, "Amyr, this boat did not break loose by chance. God was letting you know something was wrong on board."

It has, in fact, been a warning. If PARATII had not broken loose, we would not have seen the fire in time. I look to the wind for a second, then look upward and give thanks.

I knew about this risk from the outset. The South Shetland Islands, except for Deception Island, are a challenging archipelago for small vessels. The islands are still subject to the influence of Drake Passage weather systems and the depressions that roll in from the Bellinghausen Sea. On the Pacific side, distances between the few existing bays are significant, with frequent williwaws that blast down from the glaciers. Also, the bottoms of these bays are not very good anchoring grounds. It is surprising to discover how little is known about the bottom of Admiralty Bay.

Sub stays on PARATII with me for two hours. We sail somewhat desperately, without raising any sails, propelled only by the engine and the windage of the mast itself.

Twice I attempt anchoring. Once in front of the station, then a second time at Copacabana, farther south. After my third attempt, I give up. No matter what I do, the gusts cause the anchor to drag. The windlass proves reliable, even as it releases then hauls in hundreds of pounds of chain. If it had failed I would have to sacrifice the anchor and head out to open water. But I can't entertain thoughts of leaving now. After all, I would be kidnapping an officer of the Brazilian Navy!

Sub, completely soaked, is tireless and insists on spending the night aboard, helping me control PARATII. Still, I ask him to leave. It is safer. If all else fails, I can always make a run for it, even if I am unsure about where I'll go. What I am sure of is that I won't sleep until the wind lets up. Gee, if I had only known how precious those last hours of sleep were to have been . . .

By radio we once again call for Boat Number One. Once again the mad rush: into the incubator to clamber into the survival suits, haul out the boat trailer, wade through the waves, yank on the pull-cord to the 50-horsepower outboard. Once again the boat makes its way out and retrieves Sub.

The cold, dark night wears on. The wind continues to shriek. I am alone, dazed, soaked, and black as coal. I also discover that at some point during all the dashing about to put out the fire, my beloved knit cap vanished. Now, I miss that cap as I would a precious jewel, though I don't believe much in amulets or luck.

Speaking of luck, other than a smoky interior, my situation is not actually that bleak. I was just scared. PARATII kissed the rocks but did not run aground. Nothing was broken and the engine is working. What I need now is simply to summon up the energy and poise necessary to keep the boat pointed straight into the violent gusts, and the patience to wait for the sun to rise again.

It is the eve of Carnival. No doubt, all of Brazil is dancing in the streets, having a blast. And I am dancing too, just to keep my body warm and stay awake. I would love to change clothes but I don't dare let go of the helm. Every now and then I spot ice, a few feet away from the bow. At other times, powerful wind gusts blow spray off the surface, hosing me with salt water. It is a night of pure horror. Many times during those endless hours of darkness, I try unsuccessfully to anchor PARATII. Outside, all I can see are the confusing lights of Ferraz Station, and nothing of the rocks or ice chunks passing alongside.

In all, I make eleven attempts in eleven different spots. I go out to the bow each time the anchor is hauled back in. Twice, while retrieving the anchor, I must step off the bowsprit, and scale down the chain itself. Standing on the swinging anchor, holding onto the chain with my left hand like a monkey on a vine, I use a machete in my right hand to hack away tons of tangled algae.

Panic? No. I passed that stage a long time ago. The situation is becoming funny. By the tenth time I drop the anchor, while using the lights on shore to gauge how fast the chain is running out, I notice that on the deck and bowsprit I have collected enough marine samples from the depths of Admiralty Bay to attract the jealousy of scientists who come here for that specific purpose. My headlamp illuminates mud, rocks, algae, and small critters dredged up from the deep.

Early in the morning, still shrouded in darkness and trying to hold the boat still, I suddenly start running down the deck like a miner escaping an explosion—to answer a VHF radio call from Commander Aquino. He is objective and straightforward, and calms me down. These winds will be here a while longer. I should be patient and calm. It might even get worse. This means more of the same: I could either stop the engines or sail over a tight area, making constant maneuvers. For the ships Aquino commands around here this is mere routine.

He tells me it would be highly risky to seek shelter in another bay, in the dark, and advises against it. Any other bay would also have large glaciers and, if the wind clocks around as it always does, I will be trapped by ice on one side, pressed inward toward rocks or the glaciers themselves.

That call comes in before Anchoring Attempt Number Twelve. Commander Aquino suggests dropping a second anchor. I have already considered this option, but if the anchor line to the second anchor fouls the chain to the first anchor, I'll be in a real mess. Squatting, I cross the deck and untie the 100-pound "mercy" anchor, my last resort. I take it up to the bow and then, while struggling to keep my ears warm under my foul-weather hood, I have an idea. Instead of dropping the anchor on its own line, I decide to use shackles and six feet of chain to attach the second anchor in tandem with and behind the main anchor. Now, that's an easy idea to come up with, but it's much tougher to execute under conditions that send shackles flying everywhere. I have the distinct impression that with every gust of wind I am performing an aerial lift-off, right from the deck. The danger is that if my idea doesn't work and I need to haul everything up, I will be unable to cut off the algae from the first anchor.

From my survey conducted while attempting to anchor so many times, I select the most promising ground and drop the whole arrangement in the water, again near the station. This time the anchors grab the bottom. The wind increases and, even when I put the engine in reverse to test the hold, the anchors don't drag.

Though both anchors are holding, I turn on all the alarms—depth sounder, radar, and baking timer—and, soaking wet, I jump into bed for forty minutes. Daybreak comes and brings with it a new problem: the wind, which indeed increased, has loosened the ties that hold the furled mainsail tightly to the boom. Small bits of exposed sail create earthquake-like vibrations throughout the boat. No, we will not have torn sails! Using lengths of chain attached at both ends to a line, I stitch up a chain chute, and use it to secure the rebellious sail. It is like two hours of dirty fighting. My fingers have lost all strength and feeling, making it almost impossible to tie knots. But in the end, the jury-rigged chute does its job.

Inside, I get out of my drenched clothes and put on dry ones. I am dizzy with exhaustion. Never in her life did PARATII have such a mess inside. Wet, sooty, and mud and rocks strewn everywhere. My inflatable dinghy was left back at the station, on land. It flew away several times, with its outboard attached and all, until the good folks at the station mercifully buried it. It survived.

In the morning the same group—Ricardo, Sub, Viana, and

also Gutemberg—step aboard from their now-famous Boat Number One. They insist on giving me a full drum of Petrobras diesel specially formulated for use in the Antarctic, which I gratefully accept. I've had to face many challenges with the heater and filters, because of the worthless diesel I am still carrying, furnished in Santos by an unknown distributor. How stupid of me not to insist on a guaranteed pure fuel, just because I was running out of time.

Awash in the wonderful fragrance of fresh diesel, the five of us have lunch. How thick-headed I am! I finally figure out how the fire got started: first, excessive carbonization and low-quality oil gummed up the safety float and, second, strong chimney suction.

Back at the station I am rewarded with another bath, my fourth. While enjoying the shower steam, I can't believe the agonies of the previous night are over. I am also rewarded with a bunk bed so I might get a few hours' rest, but I only manage to sleep for forty-five minutes. While I sleep, one of the men from the Ferraz Station stands watch on PARATII. Also while I am sleeping, the staff at the station decides that, despite the bad weather and rain, they want a closer look inside the boat. My goodness! When I wake up I have less than one hour to get back on board and do some chores that will break all previous Antarctic housecleaning speed records.

When the first wave of visitors arrives, I am still on my knees—buckets, washcloths, and a large brush in hand—mopping up the mess. The boat is almost back to shipshape.

When the visits are over, we go back to the station to pick up the little orange dinghy. With its motor removed, we tie it to PARATII's stern. But the party isn't over. I return to the base with the gang and, suddenly, once we are already inside, José Henrique, the guy who researches the ozone layer, sounds a new alarm. This time, it is the orange dinghy that blows off PARATII. It, too, is now headed for the Polish base, Arctowski . . .

The same orders again! Launch Boat Number One! Again, we jump into the survival suits in the 140°F incubator, leap into the freezing water, and start the outboard. Once at sea, the motor dies again. Order the rescue! Again, Boat Number Two to the rescue of Boat Number One. Boat Number Two ends up rescuing the orange dinghy before those of us in Boat Number One can get to it. Then Boat Number Two comes to our assistance, towing Boat Number One back to PARATII.

Once on board I notice that PARATII is too close to the station. Both anchors dragged somewhat with the most recent williwaws. I drop anchor again about sixty feet away, and return to the base. Next, Boat Number Two's motor dies down, and Boat Number One's, which is now working again, is sent off to rescue Boat Number Two. What to me seems like an endless adventure from hell, to the Navy's support people is just another day on the job. Everything gets handled quickly and efficiently.

Again we get into dry clothes, leaving our boots in the 140°F incubator to dry before heading off to dinner. Helena, the mountain climber, gives an engaging lecture about her climbs around the world. After a small ceremony, a low-key Carnival party begins. I excuse myself and, half-dead with exhaustion, slip out to my bed on PARATII. I have not slept in two days. Despite having to check my position every twenty minutes, I sleep like a polar bear.

The two anchors give me no more trouble, but the next day the winds grow even stronger and again a piece of the mainsail almost explodes into shreds. There is no way I can stay here any longer, not even to wait for the weather to improve. Sub and Viana come aboard to bid farewell and end up helping me haul in the first anchor, which is hanging from the second anchor. While we do this, the wind is dragging PARATII away from shore, with Boat Number One in tow. We say our goodbyes and they speed off toward shore.

When I am already far away, trying to figure out how to raise the storm trysail without dropping the mainsail, I look astern to wave a final farewell. No! Not again! One of the two men is on his feet, yanking wildly the starting cord to Boat Number One, which is quickly being blown far away. The motor died again. It is now my turn to repay them for the infinite courtesies they gave me, though my contribution is nothing compared to theirs. I bring PARATII about, circle the little boat, and cast them a line. I tow them against the wind toward the station until PARATII's keel scrapes the bottom. They are behind me, trying to get the motor to start, unable to row the boat ashore. Once again, the wind pushes them out to sea. I make a second pass and this time, with PARATII's bows over their heads, I push Boat Number One until PARATII's keel scrapes bottom again. This time they are able to row ashore.

I am no longer dizzy from exhaustion, but from the incredible succession of events—not to mention having to leave the bay under massive williwaws. I know it won't be fun once I get outside the bay. A full-fledged carnival of winds all the way to South Georgia Island, 800 miles ahead.

Only after I leave the island behind do I recognize what a cauldron of winds I was in for the past three days. It's not that the weather improves once I leave, but outside Admiralty Bay there are no more gusts and williwaws; and the waves, though large, are rather uniform. PARATII is sailing beautifully under reduced sail, heading north. The strong northeast wind is not very helpful, but at least it brings this comforting thought: all the icebergs produced in the Weddell Sea ice factory and shipped in this direction will be blown back to the east.

I find freedom on the open seas, safety, and comfort in these strong winds, free of williwaws and the hazards of land. However, in spite of everything—save for the number of attempts to anchor at Ferraz Station—every second spent with the folks back there was worth it. I leave them with a debt of gratitude I will never be able to repay and that I intend never to forget. I also will never forget that it was on that beach in front of that very station, where PARATII twice just bumped her keel, that I made the decision thirteen years ago to build this boat.

15

BY A MERE
TWENTY-FIVE MINUTES

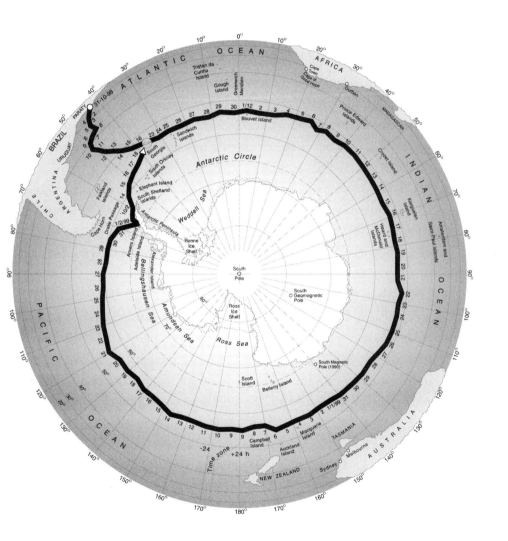

Around midnight, I pass Elephant Island, leaving it forty miles to starboard. The island is famous for having been the first island where Ernest Shackleton and his men found refuge. There is a Brazilian shelter on the opposite side where I would like to go someday. I would also love to see the shoreline from which Shackleton began the most spectacular sea crossing ever recorded. As I travel a course parallel to the one traveled by the tiny JAMES CAIRD when it sailed from Elephant Island to South Georgia, I replay in my mind the details of that epic voyage.

In recent years, groups of individuals from around the world, with plenty of bravado and nothing better to do, have attempted to replicate Shackleton's feat. Invariably, they come on comfortable ships or sailboats, rested and in good shape, armed with satellite communications, GPS, weather charts, and thermal suits (Shackleton's argonauts were on the ice for over eighteen months, shipwrecked, without ever setting foot on land). And these modern-day adventurers always arrive during the summer. Even so, they still manage to fail. Even those who somehow complete the 800-mile sail to South Georgia Island are not actually replicating anything at all. To truly accomplish what Shackleton and his crew did, they should undertake the voyage in the dead of winter, soaked, with nothing but a sextant and a waterlogged almanac. And that's just the crossing. Next, they must do what Shackleton, Crean, and Worsley did—trek across the mountains and glaciers of South Georgia Island without the benefit of mountain climbing tools.

The only beneficiary of those media-driven attempts is

Shackleton himself, probably grinning from his Grytviken grave. With every attempt, the appreciation amateurs and professionals hold for the courage that Shackleton's odyssey required can only increase.

All I want, after passing Elephant Island, is to have no odyssey to recount. Just five days to complete my dream plan, 360 degrees. Into the wind, PARATII climbs up the minutes of latitude with ease. From here forward, though the latitudes are downsizing, the frequency of icebergs pouring out of the mouth of the Weddell Sea could actually increase. I mostly don't want to make any mistakes. I call Hermann in Brazil and we agree on a new frequency for radio contacts. The weather forecast I receive is not bad. The problem is that, though I am down to the last few days before arriving at the finish line and desperately anxious to enter Grytviken, there is still a stretch of treacherous sailing to do. I am not worried about bad weather, but only with the direction of the wind and I wish to avoid adventures of any kind.

I have a long radio conversation with Brazil. By phone patch I am able to speak with the girls at home. Super América, PY2AEV, comes on next with news of friends on other boats. Márcio, in his small CARAPITANGA, is on his way to Cape Town, along 40°S. Raul and Crespo's ANNY is also headed toward the cape from the Indian Ocean. So many tropical tales on the air, but here I am, still plotting deep-freeze positions at 58°, 57°, and 56°S.

In the early hours of Mardi Gras, February 16, I cross longitude 47°30'W, the same longitude I crossed on November 9 of last year. Although PARATII has now crossed all 360 meridians of the earth, she did so in different latitudes; last year at 40°N, this year at 56°S. The route I plotted on Chart No. 4009 was shaped like a spiral, not a circle. I still need to close out the circle. The next forecast I receive is dry and objective: FEBRUARY 18, 12:00 ZULU, 50-KNOT WINDS.

"Please be westerly, at least," I mutter.

Wednesday, February 17, Marina's birthday. This time I don't forget about it. I stick a candle in the remaining piece of the Siena pie Fábio gave me for Christmas, hard as a brick at these temperatures, but the closest thing to a cake I can find down here. The Chilean Navy forecast confirms Marina's message. A strong depression is brewing in the Drake Passage, south of my position and advancing quickly. But, strangely, the winds around the system are weak, and the waves small.

Despite the low barometer, nothing is happening—an irritating situation. I would prefer a thousand times to be fighting through a hair-raising depression than to have to linger around helplessly. It doesn't take long for the wind to pick up: forty-knots, northwesterly. The sails are reduced to the last reef to avoid any drama. The pressure stabilizes at 986 millibars. "I've seen worse," I murmur to myself. Unperturbed, PARATII holds firmly on her course toward South Georgia.

At noon GMT on February 18, 2:30 p.m. Brazil time, the last waypoint, which I named SG-W, is 37.7 miles away. I have seen land from that distance many times in my life. But waypoint SG-W doesn't represent a piece of land. It is merely a reference point consisting of round coordinates—54°00'S and 38°30'W. The nearest land to the waypoint is the Willis Island Group, South Georgia's closest neighbor to the west. At that waypoint our course should turn eastward. The problem now is that our approach to South Georgia will take place in darkness that would not end until 4:40 a.m. the next day. What should I do? Wait until daylight, of course . . . or should I let PARATII run hard and shorten the night? Either way, I must spend a few hours in the dark, sailing through icebergs that bunch up around the islands. And to stay near land at the end of a journey in temperamental seas and howling winds is more challenging than it might seem.

"Forget putting on the brakes," I think. I let the boat run. Within five hours we passed SG-W.

At 6:05 p.m. the largest of the Willis Islands appears on the radar screen, nineteen miles to the south. No visibility. Damn it! I wanted to beat the darkness. Oh, if I only could! But I can't. I will have to trust the radar, keep my eyes glued on the bow every second, and use all the resources and skills I have at my disposal to avoid committing a stupid error this late in the game, even if it means standing on the bow, freezing like a figurehead with a flashlight in my hand. Say! Where is that 1,000-candle flashlight, anyway?

I go down to get it. I know I will spot large icebergs at some point, either on radar or with the 1,000-candle flashlight. A large number of bergs, sometimes tabular ones, come from the Weddell Sea and run aground around the islands. What worries me most are the small ones that come from the island itself. There are certainly thousands of them blowing out of the bays at that very moment. And there are thirteen bays before we reach Cumberland East and, finally, Grytviken. That means dozens of glaciers are putting invisible obstacles into our path.

There are hundreds of smaller bays. With the wind, and in this darkness, none could serve as possible shelter, even in my wildest dreams. Exactly to the north of the strait through which Cook passed when he explored Georgia, the depth finder registers 200 feet. Ahead of the bow lay some sixty miles of blind sailing through nighttime and rough seas before I can reach the bay I am shooting for. The waves and wind increase, as does the ache in my belly, to sight land, not to make any mistakes in my approach.

Choosing an arrival time is never a simple matter. Now is not a good time, and the weather isn't good either . . . I must be patient. I decide to hold latitude 53°45'S at least until I pass Cape

Buller and the Bay of Isles. Before darkness falls upon us completely I feel anxious, and go below to the engine room to check
on the drive shaft. I might need the engine in the fjord. Everything is in order. As I am leaving the workshop, I remember that
under the tool drawers, beneath the floor, is one of the Christmas
champagne bottles. "You managed to escape Christmas, New
Year, and even Dorian Bay, but you're not going to escape anymore," I think.

I don't know what triggers that thought. Of course, I am not
going to touch that bottle now, but later, after I have arrived. But
my intentions alone bring an immediate response. Suddenly, I am
slammed against the workshop wall. Four of the eight tool drawers come unlatched from their cabinet. All the tools flow out of
the drawers and stick to the ceiling, alongside floorboards—
and the champagne. The impact—a strange lateral blow that
makes the boat shake—causes the door to the entrance to come
unlatched and slam shut. The force of the slam knocks the door
handle off and sends it flying into the nether gloom. I am now
trapped inside.

In the total darkness of that enclosed cubicle, with my belly
against the wall, rollerblading on wrenches and tools of all
sizes, some of which fell through the opening created by the engine room door, I quickly grasp what is happening. PARATII has
capsized, or at least been knocked down. And there is no one
out there to take any recovery measures. I spend fifteen minutes
in despair, trapped by the door, trying to find a wrench that
matches the square nub protruding from what was once a door
handle. In the darkness, desperate to get out, I can't find anything. Something happened to the autopilot and the boat must
have broached, burying the mast in the water. The strange
shaking could only have been the mast breaking. My first
thought is that I need to find my large cable cutters and cut

away the stays to free the boat from its dragging mast. Then, I remember, PARATII no longer has stays. If we have been dismasted, there will be no stays to cut. And I just know we were dismasted.

"Damn door, let me out!" I shout.

The boat rights itself quickly. When it does, the drawers, tools, champagne, and all hell slide along the wall back to the floor again. The bilge boards are out of place. There is no place to ground my feet other than in that slippery mess.

"Okay. So the mast is gone. At least the boat is upright."

With a calmness I cannot explain, I pry open the door. There is no water below decks, despite the companionway having been open. No water on the table. The radio and charts are dry. But the biggest surprise of all is out on deck: the mast is standing tall, both sails in place. Water is still gushing out of the boom.

Incredibly, the autopilot managed to right the boat and get us back on course. We are once again surfing the waves as if nothing at all happened. Only the cockpit has water. The lines that normally filled the floor space of the cockpit are gone, now dragging behind the boat. Little by little I haul in all the lines and check everything. Blocks, sail slides, the windvane—nothing is missing. This is hard to believe.

I do not stay outside for long, fearing that another wave could lay us over again. The die-hard and efficient wind generator growls on, as if nothing happened, and the antenna is still in its place. I feel uneasy as I go down below and close the companionway hatch. I am exhausted. The lines dragging behind the boat have become soaked and heavy, but none of them snagged on anything. Not on the rudder, not on the propeller. It is not so much the weight of the lines that wear me out. No, this is mental exhaustion. Now I have to check everything below. No one comes through a wallop like that unscathed.

A few books from the starboard side of the saloon, the side that shot upward, are still there. But nothing else. Everything else flew to the port side. Some of the objects, I don't know how, ended up in the galley, farther aft. I pick everything up and return each item to its place. Some things, such as the batteries and chargers for the VHF radio and other cordless tools flew all the way across the saloon and somehow landed in the galley sink. Silverware, which was in the sink, is now on the floor. The indestructible wooden salad bowl I had bought in one of those Japanese stores in Liberdade, in São Paulo, broke in half. But the champagne bottle, which also went flying, is intact. I think it wisest, though I'm not superstitious in the least, to keep my distance from that bottle.

"Only after we get there. If we get there."

The radar is still working and picked up land off to starboard. I have no idea what that land is, having lost all sense of time while putting the boat back together, running up to the bow and back without stopping even for a second. Even if I lose my mast and my mind, I am determined to make it to land.

At about 1:30 a.m., while checking my position, I notice I crossed my own starting line—the line I drew when arriving at South Georgia Island back in November. I have finally closed the circle. Now, yes, the 360 degrees around the earth have been traveled. A trip around the entire world. A circumnavigation around Antarctica, only to suffer a knockdown in the final minutes! Now all I need is to arrive. I again recall the days spent with Harold and Hedel. I wonder if they are well, and what they might have been doing over the past three months.

At 3:00 a.m., it is still dark and the wind is still strong, though the seas are much smoother. Our accident must have happened when we jumped onto the continental shelf, where wave patterns change and seas become confused. These abrupt rises from the ocean floor cause more surface problems than any storm. I cannot get my mind off the incident that was almost an accident.

The Possession Bays, where Cook first came ashore fall away off our stern starboard quarter. Just ahead is Fortune Glacier and Fortune Bay. The next large bay will be Stromness, followed by Cumberland—my bay. I'd better check the engine. I release the drive shaft brake, check the throttle and choke, and turn the key. As always, she starts right up. What a comforting old rumbling sound, so secure and reliable. That sound saved me at Ferraz Station and rescued me from many jagged coastlines. It is true music to the ears for anyone about to make tight-quarter maneuvers along inhospitable shores. I rev the engine up to 1600 rpm and close (from the outside this time!) the same door that had earlier pinned me inside. As I am pulling it shut, I glance at the workbench where the drill kit was, and see—the champagne bottle. Incredible, that bottle carries some sort of power.

I barely make my way back up to the pilothouse when the engine's rpm alters ever so slightly. A chill runs through my gut . . .

"No, for the love of God, not now!"

But it happens. The engine begins to sputter. Desperately, I try to accelerate, but to no avail. When the engine stops I can't move. I am dumbfounded. The wind whistles through the sails, making the generator howl. The seas roar in seeming jubilation at my plight. That is all I can hear. I take a deep breath and attempt to gather my thoughts. Perhaps water got into the engine because of the knockdown. But how, if the engine started? If it had not wanted to start . . . Could it be air in the pump tubes? What could it be? I look at the chart. I am not about to tack my way into the bay, risking a head-on collision with glaciers. I am also not about to stay out here and wait.

I give myself a 90-minute deadline. If I still cannot identify and solve the problem, if the engine still won't start after 90 minutes of effort, then I will give up on South Georgia and head straight up for Brazil. I won't, under any circumstances, ruin the voyage by risking an approach in high winds and darkness. We are making nine or ten knots. In about 90 minutes I will be at the mouth of the bay, and will have to decide whether to enter or head back out to sea, north to Brazil.

Now, back to the engine. First I put my hand in the engine room to turn on the light, prior to entering. For the first time in PARATII's life and for no apparent reason, the light simply doesn't go on. I place my headlamp on my forehead. It was a gift from Fábio "Pinguino." Its batteries are weak. I look at the neck of the damn champagne bottle, sticking out of the toolbox, and shout, "You miserable bottle, I will drink every last drop of your contents, even if I have to go to China to do it!"

I go to get some batteries, but the box is empty. The spares are behind the locker. Under a huge pile of odd-shaped boxes.

"You're trying to test me. Very well, I'll pass your test," I mutter repeatedly.

I open a box of fresh batteries, turn on the headlamp, and tighten the elastic around my forehead. I return to the engine, adjust the wooden stool over the drive shaft, and take a good look at my hands.

"You guys have 85 minutes to make this happen."

I am able to turn the engine over manually, which tells me it is not water contamination. What could it be, then? I decide to bleed the fuel lines. This calls for three different wrenches, a $1/4$-, a $9/16$-, and a $5/8$-inch. I lean my body out of the engine room and into the workshop. Mother of God, all the wrenches, which have always been well organized, never out of place for a single day on this trip, now look like one big mess of chrome vanadium. Many of them made their way into the bilges or ended up in other more mysterious places—we're talking here of over 200 wrenches. I begin to look for the wrenches I need while sorting out the whole mess.

I don't know why, but a thought finds its way out of my mouth, in French:

"S'il faut mourir, autant le faire avec classe."

I say that inadvertently, because if I indeed would be facing death, I would fight and curse to the bitter end. I heard the phrase in French a long time ago, spoken by the mast builder as he was recounting Pete Goss's spectacular rescue of Raphael Dinelli, over Christmas 1996.

Dinelli was sailing an Open 60, singlehanded, in the ill-fated Vendée Globe race around the world, the same race in which Australia's SAR rescued Tony Bullimore and Thierry Dubois. Dinelli's boat capsized in the southern Indian Ocean. At that time, Pete Goss was farther ahead, sailing through the same low pressure system. When he heard that the Frenchman had cap-sized, he decided to come about and sail back into the wind and waves to attempt an almost impossible rescue. After forty hours and several knockdowns of his own, Goss, who was sailing a smaller 50-foot boat, found Dinelli's vessel; it was breaking apart and sinking. The Frenchman had already climbed into a life raft and was firmly clutching a package that any by-the-book mariner would presume to hold a GPS, a radio, and first aid gear.

What the package contained, in fact, was a large bottle of champagne. The Frenchman decided that if he were to die, he would die while drinking champagne . . . France's bubbly manu-facturers love to tell that story.

No Sir, not me! Not with class, not with champagne. I just want to get my engine running before heading into the bay. That's all.

I find some metric wrenches. The English ones are not to be

found. Minutes are racing by. With my fingers, I work my way to the last filter along the line before the injector pump, and I find the plastic spigot. I turn the spigot, put some of the diesel between my fingers, and taste it. It isn't pure fuel. It is salty! Phew! I spit it out. Of course! Salt water must have come in through the cockpit vent. I go to the daily tank, turn the faucet, and take a sip. This water is salty and tastes like diesel. Delicious! I know what the problem is. Now I need to fix it. I drain all reservoirs, the daily tank, and the filter, any spot that might have retained water. Air has gotten into the lines. I bleed the air until the last bubbles. Nervously, I turn the ignition. It won't start.

"Be calm, be calm!" I tell myself.

Forty-five of my ninety minutes are gone, but at least I have now identified the problem. I need only to remain calm and make no mistakes in the connection sequence. I am doing something wrong. I get out the engine manual. That's right, the manual! There is no time to trust my memory or experience . . . I open it to the Table of Contents: *Priming the fuel system*. I check the opening sequence. I repeat the operation. I get up, hold my breath, dry my hands off with a towel, and turn the key . . . VROOOM!!!

Nothing, nothing in the world could make me happier than to hear the engine once again. I can hardly believe it. I rev it up to 2200, 2400 rpms—just for the pleasure of having fixed the problem. When I return the keys to the workshop, I look at my sixty-dollar G-shock watch. Because of an oversight in my preparation, this is the only chronometer I have on board. I have 25 minutes left before the 90-minute deadline expires.

If I fail to get the engine running, it won't be a tragedy to return to Brazil. I am prepared. I have water, power, and food. I also have a double dose of homesickness for my dear girls and everyone back home. But it would be sadly ironic to complete the 360-degree turn around the earth, yet fail to reach my objective, the old and rickety wooden pier from which I departed 88 days earlier—and to miss it by a mere 25 minutes!

I step outside. It is already daylight. I put my hand on the old wooden handrail. I give it three little taps, and whisper, "We dodged that one."

I am immediately struck with a rather sad memory. Just before I departed on my trip, Harold, in his smiley and funny English, told me that if everything ran smoothly I would not return to the same wooden pier. I didn't understand. He explained to me that the government of the Falkland Dependencies, headquartered in Stanley, had already contracted an engineer and a ship to tear down the old pier and build a new one, between December and January, the same months I would be absent. So by now the new pier should already be in place. Those old cleats and pilings—with all the stories only they could tell—will be resting on a scrap heap somewhere.

I identify Stromness Inlet, Jason Peak, and Larson Point, just ahead. I take out my old Nikon F2 from its black satchel and take a photo of the bow, without moving away from the helm. The wind is so cold it hurts, but I don't want to go below. I return the camera back indoors and put on the phosphorescent orange gloves the folks at Ferraz Station gave me. These are vinyl gloves designed for heavy-duty work in extreme cold. Though the waterproof qualities of the Japanese gloves had won me over, ultimately these gloves are made of the best material I ever used for sailing.

I round Point Larson and head southward. The Nordenskjold Glacier appears at the far end of the fjord. Incredibly, the weather clears. A sliver of sun escapes from the east, shining on the island's snowy peaks and coastlines. It is a dream come true.

At 7:10 a.m., PARATII's bow reaches the wooden pier. It is the same old wood, the same old pier. The English engineer came, gave up, and returned home, leaving the pier as it was. Now, on that same old pier I had left, I hand PARATII's docking lines to a woman who stands there, smiling, observing my rudimentary maneuvers. It is Hedel.

Friday, February 19. Eighty-eight days and thirty-three minutes later, I am back. I am back with an impeccable boat that is clean, washed to the tip of her mast . . .

"Congratulations, congratulations, Amyr! Coffee is ready!"

"Where is Harold?" I ask.

"Very, very sick! In the bed!"

The MORITZ D is no more than 30 feet from us, giving me a short walk on a long pier. I board the German sailboat and find Harold hot with fever, but happy as ever. The coffee pot is leaning against the heater. He apologizes for not being able to serve me.

"Please, help yourself!"

I am somewhat thinner—and with a beard. On the outside, some differences, perhaps. On the inside, I am the happiest man on the planet, drinking the best cup of coffee I ever had in my life. Hedel, holding her own cup, stands by the companionway giggling as always, the only eyewitness of the voyage I have just completed.

16

ENDLESS SEA

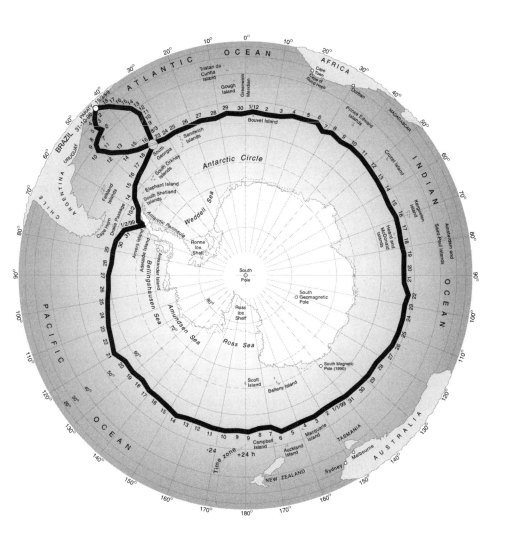

"The echo of an elephant seal!"

The deep roar reaches through the wind and across the bay. The sheets of tin covering the bone factory and the rendering houses, both in ruins, flap loudly in the gusts. Occasionally a door to the main bunkhouse, next to the Kino ("cinema" in Norwegian), swings open, and then shuts. A ghost town. Tim and Pauline Carr did not yet return from the United States. Their small CURLEW, now abandoned for the first time in many years, is still tied to the side of the half-sunk whaler PETREL, providing her some shelter. Harold and Hedel agreed to take care of the boat and its lines until the Carrs' return.

Sitting on the bottom end of a plastic container I took from PARATII I am hard at work in front of the water faucet next to the rendering house. Though I am wearing rubber gloves, my fingers are freezing. With my sleeves rolled up, I put my hands in the crystalline water. Running water, finally. Now I can wash all the clothes I wore on the voyage. The sounds of water and tin roofs, of ruins and animals—this is new to my ears. This old place is like a strange garden. Oxidizing metals look like red flowers; pieces of wood are covered with a bright green moss; a garden of rotting buildings surrounded by snow, rocks, and sea. In my short three-month absence, Grytviken has taken on a new meaning. It is a haven in Paradise.

The last time I was here, my mind was busy visualizing the challenges and struggles ahead. Now, in control of my own schedule again, I can afford to admire my surroundings, simply observing things as they are. This is not the feeling of having won a

Grytviken. The old whaling station where Shackleton is buried.

battle, of having struggled to overcome obstacles. Rather, it is something deeper, an inner peace that comes with having fulfilled a long-held dream, with having done and seen things I always wanted to do and see. It is the profound joy of having reduced my most daunting voyage to a simple circle sketched on a piece of paper; of having closed that circle in a place like this—with Hedel as witness.

The sun illuminates PARATII's white mast at the end of the pier. If my fingers were not so cold, I could spend an eternity sitting there like a laundress, absorbing the sounds of the island, admiring that red and white boat I brought back to this place—or better, she brought me here.

Back on board I take a thorough bath, trim my hair and beard. PARATII is sparkling clean. For the first time in a long while, the heater is ablaze and problem-free. A few coal marks remain to remind me of the fire back at the Brazilian base. The new diesel, sweet and clean, is burning perfectly. The saloon quickly becomes as comfortable and dry as a ski lodge. Only one area escaped my housecleaning: the aft stateroom, where I stowed the huge mainsail I removed in Dorian. I was not able to fold it properly, so I resorted to jamming it into the stateroom, which it filled all the way to the headliner. As soon as I can round up four helpful arms, I will spread it out on the pier and fold it correctly, to free up some space. The fact of the matter is that now I don't need a stateroom. I don't need anything at all.

It is rare in life not to want anything, not even time. By completing the circumnavigation in less time than I anticipated, time has been presented to me as a gift. I decide to use it to do nothing at all. I will not go anywhere; I won't count hours or days. The homesickness I feel for family and friends is not anguish, but reward, though I am not sure I deserve a reward. After all, I have only done what I always dreamed of doing. It is reward enough just to be back here in one piece, in better shape than when I left.

In the evening, after a quick QSO with Brazil, I open that old red-ribbon chocolate-looking package; the one Hedel had given me the day I departed. It is chocolate, indeed. I eat a piece and save the portion of the wrapper on which are written the words, *Bon voyage PARATII*. In fact, it was a good voyage.

Soon, it is Hedel's turn to get sick. Same symptoms: high fever and cough. I pay the couple a visit to thank them for their gift and to deliver the news that the small celebration dinner I am planning for them will be postponed until they both feel well enough to get out of "the house." I still have some wine and that tantalizing, mischievous bottle of champagne, which this time will stand no chance of escaping.

There are days of strong winds and bright sunshine. At times I even go shirtless. The heat and the impressive clouds that form over Cumberland Bay come with successive drops in barometer readings. Outside, the sea must be hell. In this regard, Grytviken is a special harbor: at times it gets hammered by strong williwaws that swoop down from the mountains, but the place is invariably an oasis during truly foul weather—thus, the title of Tim and Pauline Carr's book.

Antarctic Oasis is one of those rare masterpieces of simplicity and poetry, an unusual feat, considering it was written by a couple who lives under extremely simple physical and material conditions. It is hard to imagine living on a 100-year-old boat that has no engine, no head, no electricity, and not a single technical amenity. But the Carrs are a couple committed to each other, and committed to living life in the pursuit of a joint cause. When I look at it that way, I think I can almost understand how they do it.

Harold and Hedel—white-haired, smiling, and serene—also live in a small boat. The MORITZ D is much more practical than the Carrs' CURLEW. It is built of unpainted aluminum, has an engine, and radiates a voyaging spirit. Without a drop of heroism or fanfare they travel, stopping along the way to work just enough to keep going. Harold is a professional carpenter and Hedel a retired physician who learned how to build, paint, and weld so she could sail. Taking unconventional routes, they circled the planet twice. Drawn onto the inflatable plastic globe they keep on board are daunting routes that would send chills down the spines of experienced captains, though they never boast about their feats, and never mention the notion of adventure. Casual and artificial terms like "adventurer" or "explorer" fail to define Harold and Hedel. They simply do what they enjoy—sailing on their own, accompanied only by enormous mutual respect and courage. I deeply admire those two. To hear them say on my arrival, in a German accent, "Amyr we are proud of what you did," is the greatest homage I could have been paid. Nothing on the planet—not prizes, money, trophies, titles, or any other banner or coin, the rewards that often drive human endeavor—could be worth their simple acknowledgement of what I have accomplished.

I still have homage of my own to pay. When I return to
PARATII I pop the cork on that damn champagne bottle that has
been harassing me all along the journey. I serve it into four crystal goblets, then toast Marina and the girls. The next such celebration, the second bottle, still hidden below the AC/DC inverter
bracket, will only take place after the anchor is set in Brazil.

It feels strange to enjoy such a state of wellbeing and momen-
tary freedom from the calendar. For eighty-eight days I lived
under intense pressure. During that time, the greatest challenges
were not exhaustion and small hardships (cold and discomfort,
though even these were not too bad for such a lengthy trip). What
was really tough was the mental fatigue—not knowing what will
happen in the next minute, unable to relax for a single second,
certain only of the remaining cold, distance, and months ahead.
But all the pressure, exhaustion, fear, doubt, and anxiety vanish
the moment I finish tying off PARATII's lines to the ancient cleats.
Not even the slightest sign or shadow of fatigue remains once I
jump down to the pier. If only I could manage to walk in a
straight line, no one would ever guess I am coming ashore after
almost three months at sea. It doesn't take very long to regain my
land legs. The only noticeable after-effects of my journey are that
I am a few nights behind on sleep, my left ear still bothers me a
little, and I am more physically fit than ever.

Harold recovers from his fever. He plans to restore the hy-
draulics system in the Old Bunk House and install a sewage system. I volunteer to dig ditches for laying the pipes. I desperately
need to throw myself into some sort of land-based work. There
isn't much to do on PARATII other than fold the mainsail. The only
physical damage I have to show for my trip is on the soles of my
feet. Walking is painful for quite some time. But digging ditches
with a pick and shovel causes no discomfort, though I am sur-

prised at how rocky the soil is. Within minutes, I shed both sweater and jacket and am down to a T-shirt.

I spend entire days digging with a pick, gazing at the solid ground I did not see for so long, thinking about nothing. My best days are spent in Grytviken busting up rocks and digging long trenches—hours of silence punctuated by lengthy conversations during tea breaks. My hands become covered with blisters and calluses; the soles of my feet are recovering. Within a few days I become an experienced ditch digger.

Two new boats show up at the dock. First, a French sailboat from New Caledonia, owned by a solitary, heavily bearded man named Vincent. The second is a tiny but famous wooden boat, WANDERER III, making its fourth journey around the world. Arriving from Stromness, to the north, she is being sailed by Thies Matzen and his wife Kicki, a fun and lively couple. During my absence they got married in a little church Hedel recently restored. I think that was back in December. They even "imported" a priest and reception supplies from Port Stanley. Their plan had been to winter in Grytviken, with WANDERER III in the bay, encased in ice. But the boat was so tiny they had been unable to load enough kerosene and coal to last a full year, so they gave up on that idea. Now, they will be leaving in a few days, though they have yet to decide on a course, whether to head upwind back to the Falkland Islands or farther east, to Cape Town. The wind will make that call.

Vincent, on the other hand, has no doubt about what to do with his life. Sailing a boat he built himself, he is a far cry from those self-acclaimed "adventurers," but instead, a model of competence and good sailing sense. He went down to the Antarctic Peninsula with his wife and daughters, one month before I arrived. After unloading the family in Ushuaia, he is now headed back to his Pacific home in New Caledonia, singlehanded. He, too, is concluding a circumnavigation. His plan is to travel along latitude 42°S, making no more stops.

During my long conversations with Harold and Hedel at the end of each work day, we discuss boat construction. For example, WANDERER III was a pioneer design back in a time when it was rare for a family to cruise the world in a sailboat. Today, tens of thousands of families are doing just that. Some of those cruising families have grown bored with the social and bureaucratic routine found in the conventional, touristy routes that run through the Panama Canal and the tropics. So many sailors now seek destinations that see fewer visitors but are rich in wildlife and virgin nature. The Far East, the Aleutian Islands, the Amazon region, Patagonia, and Antarctica are those kinds of destinations. What is a bit unusual is that the overwhelming majority of boats that visit those places are home-built. Individuals or families, who wish to sail the world by sailboat, rarely purchase their vessels ready-made. They build their own, and money becomes a lesser concern. For sailors in these latitudes, the critical assets are skill and craftsmanship—possessing them and improving them. Every sailboat is a treasure trove of solutions and ideas to be studied. I love to snoop around boats, asking questions, and learning from people who really know what they're doing. Harold's boat is a treasure chest of good ideas, and I pay frequent visits to CURLEW.

Vincent tries to leave the day we finish the sewage ditch. The sun is spectacular but the heat ominous. As soon as he reaches the open sea, he runs into 50-knot winds and seas white with spume. He comes back in, to depart the next day. Thies and Kicki, after working hard to reduce the weight on the overburdened WANDERER III, also leave.

I plan to stay in Grytviken until March 5. Hermann received a new Iridium phone. He wants to test it and insists that I wait while he produces a volunteer who will deliver it to me. He tried to send the device on the CALEDONIAN STAR (the same ship I ran into in Dorian Bay, now on its way here from Ushuaia) but there hadn't been enough time. The only possible ship, the venerable old EXPLORER, recently renovated, will depart in ten days. Three volunteers jump at the opportunity to bring me the phone: Júlio, who just returned from a cruise on KOTIC that ended in Ushuaia, and Breno and Edu, two friends from Rio. All three are photography junkies who can't resist an opportunity for great wildlife shots. The plan is for EXPLORER to make a quick trip to South Georgia, where it will drop off the three Brazilians on King Edward Point, near my position. Thirty-three hours later, she will pick them up in the dark, at sea. This has the makings of an interesting rendezvous.

On the evening of March 25, as planned, CALEDONIAN STAR anchors at South Georgia, a stopover that lasts only a few hours but gives me the chance to reunite with the ship's crew, take another hot shower, and eat dinner aboard. After dark, while I await Suzana's tender, which will return me to PARATII, I make the most surprising find of my entire voyage. As the tender is being lowered from its davits, with Suzana aboard, I stand waiting next to the door of the CALEDONIAN's boathouse. Where I stand, there is a glass-top counter. I am alone. Prompted by some unknown urge, I press my forehead against the glass to see what is inside the counter. I almost fall over backwards. Lo and behold, my filthy, beloved wool cap bearing the yellow letters that spelled "Yelcho" is in that counter, folded in half. Someone from the ship must have picked it up along the way somewhere. I don't have time to ask who found it, or where. I reach behind the counter, grab the cap, pull it onto my head, and jump into Suzana's tender, which takes me home under a spotlight beam. To this day I have no idea what journey that wool cap must have taken to wind up back on PARATII.

Now that the digging is finished, and my feet have healed, I begin to make long meandering visits into the surrounding mountains—proudly wearing the prodigal blue cap. South Georgia's geography is spectacular. It goes without saying that the price one must pay to enjoy this complex of stunning natural beauty and wildlife—treacherous weather—is more than fair. The weather on the island at the moment is challenging, not because of snow flurries and gales, but rather because of a strange, oppressive heat that generates fierce winds and seas out beyond the bay. It is very unusual to feel this kind of heat wave on South Georgia Island. Meanwhile, I am happy to bask in the sunshine, barefoot and shirtless in the midst of patches of snow, though I know I will have to pay for these vicarious pleasures, just as soon as I leave the island.

On March 5, precisely at 1:00 p.m., EXPLORER arrives and dispatches the three Brazilians in a zodiac. At midnight the following day, a Saturday, she fishes them back out of the water. It is a quick and hectic visit. We go out in PARATII a few times, take some photos of the island's largest glacier, and then I don my tour guide hat and take them to visit Shackleton's grave, some ruins, and the church. Unfortunately, we don't have enough time to play soccer on the splendid field behind the Kino. My three friends depart just as the barometer succumbs to a freefall. And this strange heat.

I am unable to sleep. On Sunday morning, with their usual intuitiveness, Harold and Hedel figure out that I am about to leave. They are both standing next to PARATII, holding the camera, bearing small gifts and a package of fresh eggs. It is not a good time to head out to sea; I know that. There must certainly be a respectable gale blowing out there; I can sense it because of the heat. But at least the wind won't be on our nose; it will be west or southwest, exactly what I want. Later I learn that EXPLORER ran into that same storm, head-on at full force, making only one knot, its passengers all strapped to their berths and getting sick while waves hammered the ship's hull.

Departures are always tedious and tense. I leave Grytviken with mixed feelings. I am bidding farewell to some people I greatly admire, and to some of the best days I have ever spent on earth. However, special days and conquests are no good at all if you cannot enjoy sharing them with loved ones back home. Over 2,000 miles separate me from home. Even if I completed one hundred circumnavigations, nothing would matter again until I sink my feet into the sands of Jurumirim. I guess my aunt and uncle in Lebanon had a point when they were asking me, "But, son, what is the purpose of those trips of yours?"

I can't say that any particular purpose is served, nor any useful result derived from traveling months on end toward the single objective of returning to the original starting place. However, my useless circumnavigation has been my most satisfying achievement. It's hard to explain. There are mountains of useless milestones in the history of mankind, seemingly pointless feats whose importance lies merely in their completion, the symbolic value of having brought a dream to fruition. So to carry out this voyage to its end is now my most important task. It is not enough that I covered 360 degrees in a region so far from home. I have to return, hug my family again, thank those who helped me, make good on my obligations.

As I leave South Georgia this Sunday, March 7, under a bright sun and extraordinarily strong winds, I think of another possibility. If I could reach Brazil before March 25, I could be with my daughters on their second birthday. My wait for EXPLORER, at first, made me give up on that possibility. But now, after running the numbers again, if I manage to improve our performance in the crossing . . . it just might be possible.

From a technical standpoint making it home in time for their birthday is not a priority, but I know how wonderful it will feel to be there. At 9:00 a.m. I wave toward the pier for the last time. At 10:00, at the mouth of the bay, the wind is already above fifty knots, spewing ice out of the bays. It is difficult to see; the sun is in the northeast, shining on white ice that floats in a carpet of white foam—reflecting the bright glare into my eyes. The sea is covered with foam, looking like a herd of sheep, though it is still protected by the mountains. As we increase our distance from that protection, the seas begin to build. I figure the strong wind must be the result of acceleration as it comes down the island, but I am wrong. In my log, I only have the courage to enter a single line: "*Hell of a thrashing; seas have the whiteness of wind-blown steam.*"

Though the shards of ice, indiscernible in the foam, are slowly thinning out, we bump into them at least five or six times. I do not want to look back to bid farewell to the island. Waves are hitting us from the side as we head north. I feel dizzy whenever I look to the east. If I would run eastward with the wind, I would start yet another trip around the world. But this is over. It is time to head home.

With winds over fifty knots, blowing steady all night long, PARATII sails beam-on to the waves, heeled over to more than twenty-five degrees. Perhaps I should switch to the storm trysail, but she is galloping just fine with the mainsail fully reefed. I want to gain latitude.

What I gain is fear. On Monday morning the wind, a pure westerly, reaches 60 knots. The sea is violently chaotic, though my red locomotive keeps punching right through. The bow disappears in horizontal jets of spray.

At 1:40 a.m., I hear a new noise besides the slamming hull and the groaning mast bearings. It is coming from the bow and sounds like a mechanical pylon driver. I turn on the spotlight, but the light bounces off the white foam, making it impossible to see anything, not even the boat.

"Damn, what could be banging out there? I have to go outside."

Readying myself for the soaking I am sure to face, I nervously step outside, waterproof flashlight in hand. I inch my way along the lee side of the deck. When the first cascade of freezing water pours down my neck my first reaction is a primal urge to curse. "Who the hell invented sailing . . ."

"Our Lady of the Endless Sea, the anchor is gone!"

No, it can't be. I wait for a calm between two gusts, hoping for a chance to shine my flashlight on the tip of the bow. I stay flat on my belly, clutching the large spool of line near the foot of the mast. The beam of light shoots through the spray and onto . . . oh, I see. The chain is still here, but it broke loose from the windlass and runs out a few feet. The anchor was detached from the bow roller and, with those few feet of freedom afforded by the chain it is now surfing and diving through the water, making impressive arcs that at times bang against the hull and at others slam all the way up on deck—a hundred pounds of sharp steel hammering my dear boat at will.

"Oh, no! What shall I do?"

I should have used the safety harness, but there is no way to attach it while giving myself enough room to dodge the 100-pound anchor that is flying around like a giant bat out of hell in the darkness. I don't have time to return below to calmly ponder a solution, such as maybe using the windlass to shorten the chain. That is impossible. It would mean loosen the propeller shaft and turning on the engine. By the time I do that there will be 150 feet more of chain to recover. I can't slow down PARATII either. The winds are at sixty knots and she is already sailing under as little sail as possible. If I slack the sails at all they will flap themselves to shreds. So, like a guerilla warrior, I head out to the bow. If the sharp points of that damn anchor manage to gore me, I'll be dead just like that. But if the anchor were to strike a hatch, or puncture the hull, death will come more slowly. What a choice!

Though my fingers are numb, I manage to press a link of chain onto the windlass locking tab, but with every violent wave striking us, the link slips off again, allowing the chain to run out a little farther, which only make the steel arcing movements all the more spectacular. I grab a ten-millimeter line from out of nowhere and try to tie a link of chain to the locking tab. Working with one hand, because the other one prevents me from lifting off the deck like a helicopter, I am unable to tie a simple knot. The spray is blowing so powerfully I can feel cold water running down my back, making its way into my pant legs, and filling my boots.

"Holy shit, what's happening here?"

By the time I manage to lock the tab, I am worn out. The anchor looks like a grenade attached to the end of a whip laying into PARATII as hard as it can. Now I have to figure out how to haul in that monster.

I try to pull the chain in with my hand. Suicide. My upper body is yanked over the railing, but somehow I bend my legs at the knees, my calves wrapped around the steel lifeline cable, barely averting a man-overboard tragedy. I never had to use so much effort as I do in those next few moments, trying to lift myself back on deck. Each attempt to pull myself up is accompanied by shouts and grunts—when I am not spitting out mouthfuls of saltwater.

Back on deck and not wanting to kill myself, I look again for a solution. I am able to pull the chain sideways, a few inches for only a few seconds, but I do not have the physical strength to hold it or tie it off.

The line! The little red line! I have an old piece of line from Cordoaria São Leopoldo. It is easy to work with and I always kept it tied to the cleat, just in case of an emergency. I tie one of its ends to the locking tab. I thread the other end through one link of the chain. And pull. Pulling and threading, pulling and threading, link by link, praying that the anchor won't impale me or puncture the boat. I handle the chain for a full hour until, finally, I am able to grab the anchor flukes and haul it aboard. All the strength in my hands is gone, so I use my forearms to hoist it into place. Using a *carioca* knot, I tie it as well as possible, and then drag myself back into the pilothouse. Though I sailed over 14,000 miles through the most hazardous oceans of the world, the combined soakings along my voyage don't add up to the number of times I've been dunked in the past hour.

When I come inside I have no strength left to sit or to remove my clothes. The floor is flooded in seconds. My arms are shot. A dozen times I considered the possibility that I would sail back to Brazil with the wind on the nose or out of the northeast. I should have removed the heavy anchor and chain and stowed them below to improve the boat's stability, but I've been so lazy during the languid days in Grytviken. This latest insane battle has been the punishment for my laziness, and the fact that I never encountered this problem before. The cruel irony is that just before departing Grytviken I stepped onto the anchor and said, "The next time I lay my hands on you will be in Brazil." Though the gale let up a bit the next day, Friday night, March 12, at 42°S, well above the Antarctic Convergence, the anchor keeps jostling out of place, so I have to lay my hands on it one more time.

The water temperature hits twenty degrees, like a delicious tub of warm water. If those who sail south fear crossing below 40°, for those of us sailing northward, crossing from 60° up to 40° is like finding Paradise. Actually, I have always considered those stories of the "roaring forties," "screaming fifties," to be a silly exaggeration. It is not uncommon for tropical latitudes to get hit by nightmarish weather systems, perhaps even more hazardous than the fierce gales that strike at latitudes 70° or 75°. Even calms can be more frequent in the high latitudes.

This time, however, our passing of latitude 40° is traditional.

When the storm ends, the sun comes out, unbelievably large in the sky. The sea turns smooth and the northwest wind allows me to follow an almost perfectly straight line toward Rio de Janeiro. Rather than getting caught off guard by any more mayhem on the bow, I remove the chain and anchor and send them both below. The transfer of links and irons concluded, the day is coming to an end under a still-bright sun, so I remove my clothes. Wearing nothing but my wristwatch, I stand my watch on deck.

Sunday ends a full week at sea, the most trying week of the entire voyage. Not even during the pandemonium south of Tasmania did I suffer so much physically. Back then, I hardly ever got wet while handling the boat; and PARATII never took such a violent pounding by the waves. This time, there are scars. The sharp points of the anchor flukes left marks on the hull and deck, the spray ripped the non-skid off the bow, and a few sail slides have been damaged. But this is it. Despite contrary winds, we covered 1,200 miles in seven days. That's a good average. I am starting to believe that I might actually get to eat *brigadeiros* [Brazilian birthday party sweets] with the girls on March 25, maybe even before the party begins, if we can avoid the doldrums.

Using América's parallel frequency system, I once again speak with ANNY and CARAPITANGA. Raul and Crespo are now in the middle of the Atlantic Ocean, on their way to Brazil, headed back to Guaratuba. Márcio is still on CARAPITANGA, returning to Santos from Cape Town, by way of Trindade Island. Another Brazilian singlehander, Gaúcho, on the sailboat TAIÚ, is sailing from Martinique to Fernando de Noronha, upwind and up-current from the Guyanas. América, indomitable in her skill at arranging transoceanic radio contacts, monitors the positions, messages, and weather for all four boats. Raul raised Europe on his radio, picked up weather forecasts from Meteofrance, and relays them to the rest of us.

Less than a thousand miles to Jurumirim. The position of the Southern Atlantic anticyclone system trapped the two sailboats coming from Africa in a large band of doldrums, while giving me favorable winds. During the night I pull on my old red jacket. No more endless layers of shirts and T-shirts. The cold-weather gear, piece by piece, finds its way back into the aft stateroom, into bags, not to come out anymore. With following seas and a dry deck during the day, my only clothing is a pair of shorts. To feel heat again is divine.

At noon on Monday, with only 850 miles to go, a ship headed toward Cape Town crosses our bow, moving slower than normal. "Iceberg of steel," I think, "with people inside and smoke billowing out." It is one mile away, but I see no flag and don't even inquire about its origins.

Signs keep appearing, indicators of our drop to lower latitudes. The cape pigeons vanish, as does almost every other species of bird—petrels, Wilson petrels, and the little grey gulls. All gone. I know that in a short while the albatrosses will leave, too, for their kingdom of uninterrupted waves. I am a tropical being, to my bones, but despite the comfort I feel in the new-found warmth, what impresses me about the sea itself is its emptiness. Whales, seals, and southern elephant seals are wise to choose as their roaming grounds the colder, richer waters of the south.

While I am pondering the exuberance of life and movement

to which I became accustomed, now falling farther and farther astern, to my surprise a cloud of small fish appears in the sky about six feet in front of the bow, against the wind. "Flying fish," I think immediately. "But, so fat and slow? No wings?" No, these are not fish. My God, this is a cloud of flying squid! A bunch of them land on the deck.

Instead of running up to see them, I run below to grab a skillet.

"Good Lord, and I haven't had lunch yet!"

Twenty-three hefty squid appear on the menu, having left black ink-stains on the deck.

As Monday, March 15, comes to a close, following the squid feast, I point the bow toward the final waypoint of the journey: 23°13'S—44°41'W, the same waypoint I marked on October 30 of last year. No more corrections for magnetic deviation and no more great-circle routes or alternate waypoints. We are now on a rhumb line straight for Paraty. The wind freshens without clocking, still out of the southeast. Any available sail is run up the mast. After so much violence, I am impressed with the condition of PARATII's sails. Other than the missing sail slides, they are as good as new. I decide not to waste a single second, not to be stingy with even a yard of sail—anything to get there faster.

The last leg begins, the final five hundred miles.

"It's crunch time, *pooower* through the stroke, dig in on the *ooooars!*" I shout, on Thursday, imitating our rowing coach, Mr. Arlindo, at the end of our eight-man crew races in the canal at the University of São Paulo. That's how he used to yell. Marcão was coxswain, I was the "seven seat." Hermann, in the "engine room" could still manage to yell, the entire boat groaning under the strokes of eight oars propelling the hull, as sweat gushed into our eyes and our noses ran. The difference was that back then we were dealing with meters, not miles; and we had a coach who, by yelling insults and praise, was able to draw out that last drop of effort needed to cross the finish line in first place. Often it was second or third place, though in those final seconds it really didn't matter. The greatest exertion was not targeted at rival boats, but inside the boat itself: don't choke the oar, don't lose control of your breathing, rhythm, and balance. "Sustain the effort." Interminable seconds that always left me deaf from exertion and blind from sweat. All I could see of the coach were his neck veins pumping and the spray of saliva every time he yelled his often unintelligible urgings, until I heard the gun at the finish line, and the cheering fans of our club.

There is no shouting on PARATII, nor fans or cannon shot, but the tension building as I near the finish line is roughly the same. Brazil draws closer by hundreds of miles, not meters; and by days, not seconds. Honestly, I am tired, but I have no intention to rest until the anchor takes hold at home. Any mistake or breakdown at this late hour would be ridiculous. It would ruin the whole trip.

Marina knows this. We could have talked until the Iridium phone melted, but I decide to go silent. I will only communicate my arrival date once I am certain. It will be Sunday or Monday, March 21 or 22—if no problems pop up before that.

It is hard to conjure up images of Brazil, Ilha Grande Bay, or the green shoreline and forests of Paraty. Little half-moon bays within the larger bay, and islands cloaked in lush vegetation all contribute to make that harbor unique. I try to imagine the wild vegetation, the large trees, the imperial palms in the town square, and the trees I planted behind the house in town.

I once took hundreds of native tree saplings from Jurumirim and planted them in the city, rare trees that were once used in the construction of canoes and oars. I think of the coconut tree and palm nursery behind Hermann's house. I fall asleep thinking of trees.

Just prior to my first trip on PARATII, when I was living in São Paulo, we decided to move our office to a lovely old house on a roomy plot of land. The closest thing to a tree on the lot was a drab grey radio tower and two evergreen trees that were not very tall. The place was rather arid. Plants and flowers would not be enough to counter the impersonal drabness of a big city like São Paulo. Though I had no specific plan in mind, I made a trip across town to *Ceasa*, where I haggled with a Japanese man and ended up owning a truck full of saplings that had been too large for him to sell. I love trees, the larger the better, so I couldn't resist.

A few days later, while I was dealing with a slew of stressful situations at the office, the Japanese fellow showed up with his delivery. I was buried in hundreds of important appointments, red-tape problems, expired licenses, invoices, bill collectors, and errand boys—all demanding answers from me—and here's a Japanese man at the door with my saplings, asking for payment.

The skies darkened and a torrential rain began to pour. Wanting only to avoid having a nervous breakdown, unable to run away from the office, and with no one to help me unload the truck, I stripped off my shirt in front of everyone and began dragging the saplings in the middle of the downpour. Hermann and Edu pitched in, digging holes in the soggy earth. We were up to our necks in red mud. Everyone else left without a word, befuddled at what they saw us doing.

Eventually, with time, all those pending problems got solved, and today those trees are perhaps the densest concentration of foliage and wood in the entire neighborhood. That was the finest bit of office work I've ever done—planting thirty-four trees—though on that day it seemed an act of pure insanity, flailing around with a hoe and shovel, my hair caked in mud.

In Paraty most of the species we're accustomed to seeing are "botanical outsiders"—*Roystonea oleracea* palms, coconut trees, *chapéus-do-sol,* mango trees, *jaca* trees, and so many other species brought in over time. It doesn't matter, because there are also many exuberant native species: *ingá,* cedar, *canafístulas, caubis*—from which we slowly grow saplings so we can someday, hopefully, assist in a "botanical explosion" that overtakes the streets, backyards, and the bay itself.

I dream of seeing a tree again. The only tree on board, other than the tiny plastic Christmas tree Sérgio gave me, is PARATII's mast. Strange tree, that mast; an outsider species in its own right, with only two branches, two halves of the boom along which I pace restlessly, hoping to spot a ship or land, either of which I expect to see very soon.

On Thursday, March 18, I discover that the mainsail cunningham broke, a thin line used for trimming the sail. Nothing serious. I spend the night outside studying the stars, unable to sleep. At 3:30 p.m. on Friday, the wind dies, just as I doze off. The sails flap and the unsupported boom swings back and forth. I disengage the windvane autopilot, turn on the electronic autohelm and start the engine. Patience. Under this unbearable heat, I would have preferred not to start the engine, but with less than two hundred miles to go to reach the coconut trees on Joatinga Point, I am not about to stop, even if it means installing a stern oar on PARATII.

It turns out to be unnecessary. The engine runs for just an hour before the wind picks up again, at first on the nose out the north, then at an angle, from the northeast. The wind freshens, allowing us to clip along silently at nine knots, sails well-trimmed. This might be my last night at sea. The nearest land is Cabo Frio, east of Rio. During the night I tighten the course toward Ilha Grande, farther west. The wind holds up all night.

At 9:15 a.m., on the last day of summer, I plot Joatinga Point at 47.9 miles away, dead ahead, though I have not yet seen any land. At 9:22, standing on the boom, scanning the horizon, I almost explode: "Land ho! Land ho! Land ho! It's Brazil!"

It is Brazil, but I am not sure what part. A tenuous shadow reveals, to my right, land shapes that, because of the heat, are not even touching the horizon. I figure it for a peak on Ilha Grande, in my beloved bay, my adoptive land.

Thirteen days, zero hours, and twenty-two minutes after last seeing the glaciers of South Georgia, here is land again. On one of América's secret frequencies, I tell Marina I will drop anchor at home early on Sunday, and that until then I will maintain radio silence. At 10:05 a ship crosses the bow, heading from west to east. At 11:42, I pass another ship, this one at anchor—twenty-nine miles from Ilha Grande—now that's strange.

Uh-oh! I rerun the numbers. I confirmed that I would arrive in Paraty at night. I wouldn't see anything, not mountains, coconut trees, or any of the rich vegetation that distinguishes this region. No, I had better spend the night in some deserted place so I can set the anchor in daylight. I want to skinny dip and bid a decent, peaceful, and calm farewell to this house I've lived in for so many weeks now.

In order to take advantage of the remaining sunlight to set the anchor, I will have to stop on the outside of Ilha Grande, on Aventureiros Beach, or maybe in the harbor that fronts the island's ancient prison. I postpone the decision until I reach the island. At 3:30 p.m., the northeasterly becomes a strong easterly. The prison bay is not sheltered, nor is it conducive to peaceful anchoring. Soon afterward, I find a beach off to starboard, empty of boats and people. I turn back into the wind and tack my way toward a patch of sand that faces west, a fine spot. In seven meters of depth, I drop the anchor. I remember neither the time nor the name of the place, just that it is the sweetest instant in my sailing life. I jump naked into the water and swim around PARATII. Later, facing west while drying myself in the warm evening wind, as if all the ordeals were only a dream, I watch the sun dip behind the mountains of Paraty.

Wilson and my sisters, Gabriela and "Cabeluda" are in Paraty, and they will certainly find out I am here. Fábio and Hermann will too, even if I arrived in total darkness. I decide to sleep at anchor, right where I am, and head home early the next morning.

At 4:30 a.m., while it is still dark, after having a cup of coffee and a piece of dried banana, I hoist the sails, weigh anchor, and sail on to Paraty. The sun rises in a perfectly cloudless sky. It is the autumnal equinox, and autumn is Paraty's most beautiful season. Of all the treats in the world, none would be more special than sailing across the bay of Ilha Grande on a day like this. The silhouettes of those two old coconut trees accentuating the elegant dorsal curve of Joatinga Point come into view like a wondrous apparition.

I hardly finish my coffee when I hear the voices of Fábio and Sérgio (of CASO SÉRIO) on the VHF radio. Suddenly, still far off the coast, I spot a bright dot moving rapidly in my direction: it is Hermann and Luís Oswaldo, shouting like maniacs, aboard the faithful orange boat. Their voices are the first to wish me a good morning.

From LA PALOMA, García sends his Asturias-accented *Buenos Días*. Júlio tosses me an apple from the deck of BRISA, Fábio's steel sailboat, still painted in an awful blue color he scrounged up from who knows where. The ice-cold apple is gone in seconds. Tigrão appears dangling from a stay on a party boat, the FRANCIS DRAKE, swinging like a monkey. People seem to be coming out of little bays, from all directions.

Outside Ponta Grossa, next to Ganchos Island, two other sailboats: a crazy trimaran owned by Johnny Ferrari, who is turning

Back home with Marina and the twins.

redder, more bearded, and more Roman by the day; and the beloved RAPA NUI, always sparkling, with Grego at the helm. Two ocean-going vessels, one built of steel, the other of wood.

"Neither Greek nor Roman," I muse. "The endless sea is Brazilian."

I round the front side of Joatinga Point and enter the little bay in front of our house. The other boats that escorted me in now fall behind. I see no sign of the girls.

"Where are they?" I shout to Tigrão. He knows who "they" are, and points immediately.

"On the beach!"

Slowly, I make my approach to the white buoy that marks PARATII's mooring in the middle of the bay. Kneeling on deck, I quickly pick up the mooring line and tie it on the bow cleat, with Luís and Hermann lending a hand.

"There! Firmly in Brazil."

I stand and, deep in the bay, on the edge of the water, on the same spot of sand from where I'd left the previous October, I see them. There they are, Marina's arms are holding the girls, Laura in one and Tamara in the other, each perfectly still, so beautiful, and wearing their little white bonnets.

So much sea, instead of separating us, brought us together again. In her 141 days of absence, from start to finish, PARATII completed her trip around the world, and returned to Jurumirim. The earth is truly round. As I think about it, it occurs to me that not once was my beloved sailboat deterred—not by wind, waves, or even hazardous ice—from making her way back in one piece, to rest again in her own bay.

Best of all is the awareness, now that I am home again and holding my three loves in my arms, that the sea around our home is indeed endless.

MARINA'S LAND LOG

From 10/31 to 11/6
FROM DEPARTURE TO ARRIVAL
IN SOUTH GEORGIA

10/31 Departure.

Amyr leaves Paraty under heavy rains, on Halloween morning. Light winds.

11/1

He calls on the telephone at lunchtime, when he is passing by Paranaguá. He has a bad sore throat.

11/2

He calls at 11:00 a.m. Two hundred miles off Florianópolis. A storm hit him during the night. Southerly winds messed up his course, forcing him to tack first toward Africa, then toward Brazil!

The first scare: he heard strange watery noises. The seas were heavy and the boat was diving into the waves. Water was coming in through an old pump in the bow. Now the problem has been solved.

11/3

Cape Santa Marta. Perhaps his South Georgia challenge will now begin. He should arrive there in two weeks. The animals show up at the end of November. The boat is in excellent shape. He is now sleeping in thirty-minute sessions. Entertainment: many dolphins surround the boat.

11/4

Amyr calls. His throat is feeling better. Today he will enter international waters.

8:00 p.m.: first contact with Mr. Ulysses, PY2UAJ.

11/5

17-knot winds out of the south. Three hundred thirty miles, on a line with Buenos Aires. He is asking for the registration number of the Magellan GSC 100. Saw his first wandering albatross! Speaks by phone with the twins. "How I miss the twins!" The Iridium phone really does work. First radio contact with Laslo.

11/8

Amyr calls and says he has seen a strange island filled with seagulls. He approaches and sees it is a dead whale.

11/9

Calls and speaks with the babies. He is about 500 miles from the coast, on the high seas. Last night he spoke with Hermann on the ham radio. He has defined his target: South Georgia Island. Light winds.

11/10

Amyr calls, in a happy mood. Spectacular surfing. The boat broke its previous speed records. Made fourteen knots in heavy seas.

11/11

He's 670 miles from South Georgia.

11/12

Amyr has not called home again. Weather reports tell me he is running into light winds. He hopes to reach South Georgia on Monday, depending on the winds.

11/13

Amyr calls on Friday the 13th. He had a big scare. Heavy seas, waves five or six meters high. He was inside the boat when he heard a sound like a gunshot. When he looked outside, he saw the boom spin almost 360 degrees (the mainsheet shackle had worked so hard, it sprung loose). Because the boat uses an Aerorig system, all the boat's strength is centered on a single point. The shackle broke in sub-Antarctic waters. "In addition to the scare, it meant one hour of hard work, but now it's better than ever." I use the speakerphone. The twins hear Amyr's voice telling them about what happened. The Blonde shouts, "Papá" and jumps around, looking for him in the telephone device. The Brunette says, "Babai!" and then, for the first time, *"Bom dia"* ["Good morning"]. Amyr can't believe it!

11/16

I still didn't know where he is, so I ask for his position. He answers, "Marina, I am at anchor in South Georgia! It's a place unlike any on the planet. Very high mountains and lots of glaciers. It is an old whaling station that has about fifty houses that date back to the turn of the century, abandoned houses. Lots of sea lions here. It's a wonderful place!

"The boat is just fine.

"After this last leg, I'm going to bed."

11/17 to 11/30
FROM SOUTH GEORGIA TO THE
GREENWICH MERIDIAN

11/17 Radio contact through Mr. Ulysses, PY2UAJ.

"PARATII is tied up at a whaling station that was abandoned over thirty years ago. It was last used for whale hunting in the 1960s, and recently served as a staging base for the Falklands War. Strong winds, lots of fog, many seal and penguin colonies."

11/18

"South Georgia is an impressive place. It gives you an idea of what the whale-hunting massacre must have been like. Total destruction! From this ghost station, under frequent snow flurries, I can see PARATII tied up next to three abandoned whalers that were hit during the war. What a sinister place! Temperatures range between 2° and 3°C. The water is very clear. This is an interesting stopover."

11/19

"One of the more interesting things about such a stopover is the people you meet. Jerôme Poncet, of the famous DAMIEN 1 and DAMIEN 2, tied up here. He lives in the Falklands, and is really very special. Years ago he was in South Georgia with his wife, for the birth of their son. To this day this remains unprecedented, to have brought his wife to this inhospitable place to give birth to a child, after having spent the winter, just the two of them, in Antarctica. So many stories . . ."

11/20

"How interesting, to hear about the lives of other people who are there, such as that German couple, Harold and Hedel, of the sailboat MORITZ D. It's interesting to see the couple sailing alone around the world, especially in these regions where the sea and wind make huge demands on body and mind. In Brazil there is still a lot of prejudice about age. I bet no one in Brazil would believe them if they told what they are doing. Tim and Pauline Carr are also there, the English couple from the CURLEW, a famous wooden boat that is over 100 years old and engineless, though it, too, has been to Antarctica. Very friendly. Harold and Hedel helped me cast off when I departed South Georgia, the only witnesses to the start of my voyage."

11/23

At 7:45 a.m. (Brasilia time), Amyr departs South Georgia. Bad weather. Heading: Sandwich Islands. Water temperature: 1.9°C. Air temperature: 4°C. Wind: 25 knots. Speed: 8–10 knots.

11/24

Amyr passed the Sandwich Islands, on his 360° Antarctic circumnavigation. Radio contact via Laslo, PY2LG, and a phone patch to MIS, where publication of the book by Luís Philipe Andres, *Embarcações do Maranhão* [Vessels of the State of Maranhão] is being announced. On the phone patch with Peter Milko, Amyr said the seas were very heavy, wind strong but favorable, and temperature was about 0°C. He congratulated them on the book and sent kisses to the twins.

Heading: Kerguelen, 3,600 miles away.

Amyr is anxious to enter the Indian Ocean (only 2,400 miles to go). Tough day of sailing. Lots of fog. He ran into two large icebergs, one visible, and the other only detected by radar. Beautiful night with an exceptional lack of wind. A group of elephant seals made lots of noise. Many *Pygocelis papua* on all sides, including some that followed the boat.

11/25

The Blonde is really missing her daddy. She constantly calls out for him, then runs around the house looking for him. Today the Brunette woke up crying, calling for him.

11/26

The boat is in good shape. Only the windvane autopilot is acting up, having already been repaired once. Thirty-knot favorable winds. He has sailed about 180 miles per day. Water temperature: between −0.6° and 1.7°C (though the water in the bilges has frozen). I sense that Amyr's mood is a bit low. It's colder even than on the Peninsula. At 03:23 GMT, he saw a large iceberg near the boat. Little visibility at the edge of the Weddell Sea. Heading: South Sandwich. Projects six days' sailing to Bouvetøya. Special lunch menu: pasta al funghi!

11/29

News from Amyr through Zé Montanaro and Braulio Pasmanik. (I think Amyr made a mistake and called Braulio the day before his birthday. That was funny . . .)

11/30 "Today I crossed the Greenwich meridian!!"

Longitude 0! This region has lots of ice (small pieces of ice about the size of refrigerators float and semi-float all around). Tough sailing. He uses the radar frequently. The sea is calmer, with 15-knot winds. The forward portion of the boom has plunged into waves several times. To keep things simple, he's cooking only one meal per day. Today he had prosciutto on the menu.

12/1 to 12/7

FROM BOUVETØYA TO THE START
OF THE INDIAN OCEAN

12/1

After heavy seas, it seems things have improved. Waves decreased as he approached Bouvetøya. Visibility non existent.

"I see Bouvetøya on the radar. The island is near, just five miles away. It's visible on the radar, but I cannot see it with my own eyes. The island is covered in heavy fog (. . .)

"Everything on board is frozen. Water is −1°C and air, +1°C. It's a good thing Hermann bought good gloves.

"Today I ate the homemade bread the German couple from MORITZ D gave me."

12/2

Very foggy. Amyr is 150 miles past Bouvetøya.

"(. . .) There is so much ice, it's absurd. It's a lottery out here!"

Amyr is forced to climb one degree of latitude, because the lower the latitude the less ice he has to contend with, smaller blocks of it.

"The boat's heater is still working, thank God, and the best invention of the century was a little basket from Paraty, which I placed over the chimney."

12/3

I keep thinking about Amyr. The sea water is very cold in that region. What little heat the wind brings condenses into fog. In fact, heavy fog! It is not easy to get wet in Antarctica. The fierce cold seems to enter your bones. Today, on the ham network run by Laslo, I feel that "the mood is great (. . .) PARATII is about to begin sailing, for the first time, in the Indian Ocean."

Current position: 52°54'28"S, 13°24'47"E. His route indicates that Amyr is trying to escape the iceberg thoroughfare. PARATII has once again broken her own speed record: 194 miles in 24 hours! Wind: 25 knots. Outside temperature: 1.7°C. Water temperature: −1°C. PARATII skips over the sea at a speed of nine knots.

"Tomorrow, if everything goes well, I should be in the Indian Ocean headed for the Kerguelen Islands. I will pass very close to them."

With the good weather forecast, Amyr hopes to recover some lost sleep and cook up a special meal from the Nutrimental pantry.

12/4

The moon appeared and the seas are smooth.

"I could even drink champagne out of a crystal glass!

"It is very cold, and the boat's water supply is still frozen. Even the toothpaste froze! Water temperature: −1.9°C. "There is a lot of ice in the water. I almost ran into a large iceberg.

"The mainsheet broke. Sailing has been tough.

"I am in the Indian Ocean, 2,000 kilometers south of Cape of Good Hope, 1,500 miles from the Kerguelen Islands."

12/6

Today he shaved!!!

12/7

Radio contact through Laslo with América, Júlio of the ABUTRE, and Camerini. The twins are there, listening to their daddy. They say, "No, no . . ." and then run around. I think they feel strange because they are not used to the ham radio station. They asked to go see Santa Claus, so we went this afternoon to see him. Amyr said he is "so homesick, it hurts." He has used these three days of calms and bad moods ("I'm glad I am traveling alone") to fix the rudder bearings (they had broken). The boat hardly moved. Yesterday, she covered sixty miles. Water: −1°C. Current wind speed: 28 knots (following!). "The worst thing here is the drowsiness. I sleep in 25-minute bits, and then I'm awake for 45 minutes, with lots to do.

"Today I saw my first whale, sperm whale larger than PARATII. It must have been about 60-foot long. It accompanied me for about twenty minutes, swimming under us, around the centerboard, and circling the boat.

"The icebergs are not as frequent here, but the quantity of small bits of ice has increased. It's 12:30 a.m. here now. It's raining hard and snowing a lot, too. The sea is phosphorescent, turning into a festival of sparkling foam when waves break. It's a beautiful show!"

12/15 to 12/17
THE KERGUELEN ISLANDS

12/15

Amyr surprised us early today, by calling home. We were worried with the silence of this past week. He is three days away from Kerguelen Islands, freezing to death. Temperature of PARATII's interior: 0°C. Even the cooking oil has frozen.

"Since I entered the Indian Ocean, the sea has been rough, with waves over fifteen meters high. I surf down the waves holding my heart in my hand, but PARATII always recovers.

"It's wonderful! There are no icebergs here, just bits of ice, about the size of the MASP [São Paulo Art Museum].

"I've been flying the storm trysail for the past five days, and the winds are holding at about thirty-five knots. I have managed an average 180 miles per day.

"I miss you and the twins like crazy. I would love to send a big hug to Tigrão. I left without bidding him a proper farewell. Give Fritz at Granja a big hug. I always think of him."

12/17

The phone rang this morning. It was Amyr, calling again! The three of us, the twins and I, were really happy. The Blonde, as always, listened without even blinking, and said, "*Baco* [boat], *Papai*," And the Brunette, who was very happy, said, "*Bom dia, papai.*" I noticed that he choked up when he heard them. Amyr is 125 miles south of the Kerguelen Island—73°E longitude, 52°S latitude. (It was 5:10 a.m. on board). Now he plans to return to higher latitudes. Everything is fine on board. He is sailing across a plateau, only two hundred meters deep, so the sea is calm. The wind has calmed down, too (about time!).

Water temperature: 3°C. Air temperature: 4°C. It's warm and the sun is out. The air is dry and Amyr feels warm for the first time since leaving Paraty. Good weather and visibility.

He said he has seen very few whales during the voyage, but many penguins, small seagulls, and now he's seeing albatrosses again. He's finding the time again to fix up his daily meals. With the seas calmer, the kitchen is pitching less.

"I've covered 6,440 miles (12,000 kilometers) since leaving Paraty, with 4,100 miles to go before I step on land again, on South Georgia Island . . . one-third of the trip complete!"

12/24 to 1/3
CHRISTMAS AND NEW YEAR'S ON PARATII

12/24

It takes a long time, but news finally arrive. Amyr calls on Christmas Eve, saying he's very homesick and promising to be home for Santa Claus's next visit.

Nutrimental prepared a Christmas dinner for him to eat tonight. They really did it right!

The wind was very strong, so in order to call he had to disengage the windvane autopilot and turn on the electronic autohelm. He is already south of Australia, almost half-way done with his voyage. Everything on the boat is in good shape. The cold decreased: 5°C. He is no longer using the heater. Says he has become accustomed to the cold.

12/26

Current position: latitude: 53°03'S—longitude: 116°E. He is about 1,000 miles from southern Australia (Perth). Soon he will cross meridian 134 and will be at the farthest point from São Paulo of the entire voyage.

"I am 14,000 kilometers from home and the boat is in good shape.

". . . getting close to the magnetic south pole, the compasses are starting to go a little crazy.

"The biggest problem now is that before I left someone gave me a book that tells of the hardships of four sailors who capsized in this area, where I am. It tells of sixty-foot waves. . . . Every time I doze off, I wake up in the middle of a nightmare!

"I am so homesick for you all. The photo album of the twins you gave me is the most important thing I have on board. Not a minute passes that I do not think of you.

"Winds almost at a standstill: twenty-five knots.

"The sea is calm, waves are about four feet. Sunny and warm: 6°C. Today I had feijoada for lunch!"

Note: perhaps as a consequence of the storm that hit the region where the Sydney-Hobart Race took place, the increased size of the waves where Amyr is, has made it more difficult for him to communicate with us. By studying the weather charts and the tracking device Amyr has on PARATII, we interpret the following:

12/27

Estimated position: latitude: 53°05'S—longitude: 118°05'E. Winds: average twenty knots. Over the next 120 hours, the winds are expected to increase to over forty knots. Waves: a splotch coming from Africa indicates that waves will increase to twenty-five feet. Average temperature: 4.41°C. Interpretation: after studying the big picture and observing low pressure systems starting at 58°S, Amyr should hold to his current latitude, only heading further south after reaching New Zealand where, instead of choppy waves and wind, he will find favorable wind and currents. He should reach the Antarctica Peninsula around 2/7/99.

12/29

Position at 05:31 UTC: latitude: 54°58'S—longitude: 128°37'E. Wind: average forty knots, following. Will remain like this for the next forty eight hours. Seas: average twenty-five feet (7.5 meters), following. A wave front is beginning, causing choppy seas. Waves expected to become more "organized." Forecast: Amyr is sailing an average of six degrees every twenty-four hours. If he keeps up this pace, he should reach longitude 134°E tomorrow, which means he will be 180° from his starting point.

As of tomorrow, he will be returning home! Half of the journey is over!

01/03

I was apprehensive, not having heard any news from Amyr since December 27. I was very worried because I hadn't heard his voice on New Year. I was hunting for Internet access in Paraty, which was almost nonexistent when, after a week of silence, the phone rings. It is Amyr (whew!). I am more and more amazed as he describes what he went through at sea during those days at the end of the year:

"It was amazing. Winds reached 120 kilometers per hour, and sixty-foot waves came at us from all sides, forcing me to stand watch on deck for fifty hours straight. The wind was so strong the sea was white.

"I am exhausted, with pain all over my body. I can hardly move. The wind was extremely strong and the waves caused me all kinds of problems. The windvane autopilot holds the boat in almost any situation, but this time, it took some time off. I was unable to use either the windvane or the autohelm. It was amazing.

"The waves took away the indestructible paddle that serves as the windvane for the autopilot that Feijó made for me. I have already replaced it.

"PARATII proved once again that she is one hell of a boat, and then some. She got submerged four or five times. If she had been a slightly more fragile sailboat, the voyage would have ended right there!

"We were surfing down one wave, I had my back to the bow, when cross seas tossed PARATII about twenty or twenty-five feet to the side.

"I had to walk out to the end of the boom in sixty-knot winds! My life was in the balance over a tiny line . . . I replaced it and have now stowed it safely down below. When I get home I'll show it to you. You won't believe it!

"I have sailed 9,500 miles so far in the voyage.

"Please thank Takako for her hard work on my meal plan. I had a great lunch today.

"Call White Martins and send them a big hug for me."

Current position: latitude: 56°S—longitude: 154°E. Water temperature: strangely, 7°C. Wind: no wind. Waves: five feet (he feels as if he is sailing in Ubatuba).

Just now, Amyr has finished repairing the damage suffered during the storm south of Australia. He's taking advantage of the calm and good weather to furl the sails and dry his socks.

01/02 to 01/24
THE ROSS SEA AND THE PACIFIC OCEAN

01/02

Amyr called!

His time zone is twelve hours ahead of us.

Position: longitude: 151°W—latitude: 55°20'S. Temperature: 4°C — the water is warm: 7°C.

He is worn out. He caught sixty-foot waves. Wind reached sixty knots. The boat got knocked down many times. Sometimes the waves came from the side. The sea was white! Message to Laslo: point the antenna to 175 degrees — above the South Pole!

01/06

20:00 UTC — Longitude: 172°57'W—latitude 57°24.48'S.

01/07

20:02 UTC — Longitude: 169°96'W—latitude 57°18.72'S.

Winds at forty knots, decreasing. Temperature: –8°C (brrrr!). Forecast: in 48 hours, winds at thirty knots, twenty-five foot waves.

He plans to remain on this latitude because of headwinds. "I haven't been able to take a bath since Christmas!"

01/08

12:00 UTC — That's weird. The Orbicomm shows his position as longitude: 174°19,38'W—latitude 57°34'S. Our forecast for his position: forty-knot winds and thirty-foot waves.

01/11

20:00 UTC — Longitude: 163°36'W—latitude 57°19.3'S. Temperature: 0°C. Water temperatures still warm: 4.5°C. Winds: thirty to forty knots.

Forecast I sent to his pager: in twenty-four hours, forty-knot winds, heavy seas, up to thirty-five feet (favorable currents). In thirty-six hours, winds at forty knots, dropping to twenty. In seventy-six hours, winds at twenty knots and waves twelve to fifteen feet (yeah!).

01/12

Position: 169°96'W—57°18.72'S. Strong wind—forty knots, favorable (pushing a bit southerly). Fifteen-foot waves. Forecast: next 48 hours—twenty knots, average.

According to the conclusions drawn in his conversation with Thierry, Amyr should be cautious around the mouth of the Ross Sea, because of the high volume of icebergs there.

01/13

20:00 UTC — Longitude: 157°50'W—latitude 57°21'S. Amyr is almost on top of the Antarctic Convergence line (the line that separates the warmer northern waters from the colder southern ones). This line rises at the Ross Sea, so Amyr will sail "at the outer limits" of the Convergence. He will run into lots of snow flurries in this region, as well as ice and icebergs. Today he covered a lot of ground: five and half degrees! Winds: twenty to thirty knots (he should have two or three days of good wind). Waves: twenty feet. He plans to anchor at Dorian Bay: ninety-two degrees to go, at an average of five degrees per day, equals nineteen days to go!

01/14

8:00 a.m. Brasília time, Longitude: 154°1'W—latitude 56°57'S. Dead calm. Skies overcast. It's colder. The wind is weak.

"The climate on board is a bit calmer.

"I slept like a baby last night for almost an hour. I haven't been eating well because the kitchen rocks too much.

"I've been picking-and-choosing out of the week's meals, so I was able to mix up the menu nicely.

"Today, everything froze on board, from the honey to the toothpaste."

Yesterday the wind got above fifty knots and waves over fifty feet! He says he is very happy with the Aerorig. It keeps the boat balanced. Only in the absence of wind, through inertia, it slams a bit much.

01/15

Today, ham operator A. Martins de Santa Maria called. He said he had been talking with a friend at 2:00 p.m. when

Amyr broke in to find out the outcome of the Mike Tyson fight! Position: 142°9'W—58°S. He said the wind is very strong there and that Amyr was unable to position his antenna correctly. Temperature: –2°C. The water and detergent froze again. The seas are rough and he is being careful not to collide with ice. The boat is very fast. Forecast: sea is calm. Wind near twenty knots. He is near the Antarctic Convergence. If he heads farther south, he will run into lots of snow and ice. He is expected to go southward only when he gets closer to the Antarctic Peninsula. Each time he enters negative temperatures, the wind chill factor (with winds at forty knots) makes Amyr feel as if it is –25°C. Heat exchange in nature occurs very quickly.

01/18

Short radio contact with Herman. Winds at forty knots and temperature is minus 8°C. He is tacking through the area because winds are shifting constantly.

01/19

Position: 141°38.92'W—57°50.58'W. Winds fifty knots and sixteen-foot waves (will increase to twenty feet). Temperature: –4°C.

He is along the tangent of a cyclone! Larger waves to the north. He is in the middle of strong winds. According to his estimates, eleven days to go before reaching the Peninsula.

01/20

Fifty-knot winds. Eighteen-foot waves. Temperature: –4°C. Article in *Folha de São Paulo* finance section: "Mega-devaluation of the *real*!"

What a coincidence. This is Amyr's third trip to Antarctica and the third time he's managed to escape an economic crisis in Brazil.

01/21

Near latitude 58°S, he ran into a strong front, while another hit him from behind. Forty-knot winds. Fifteen-foot waves. Larger waves forming. By the 22nd or 23rd they could reach fifty feet!

01/23

Amyr is 850 miles from the Peninsula and 4,000 miles from São Paulo. He called in a very good mood. The wind is calm today, with high waves. He really misses home. He took advantage of calmer winds to call some friends.

01/24

Position: 105°4'W—59°.19'S (good progress!). Everything is fine, only the weather is not cooperating. The sea is rough and the boat is rocking a lot. He spoke by radio with Júlio, who is on the Peninsula (with the gifts I sent Amyr). It is great to hear from Amyr!

01/25 to 01/30
PACIFIC OCEAN AND NEARING THE PENINSULA

01/25 (holiday in São Paulo)

No holidays for Amyr on his voyage. In fact, it has been a long time since he had a full night of "sleep in a dry bed." I keep thinking about the discomfort of sleeping only thirty minutes and waking up to find a storm "pounding at the door."

It is not easy to live with this kind of stress. But I think he has shown amazingly good humor so far, despite the many difficulties. It must be hard to understand the daunting responsibility I feel with the fact that he is in a part of the world where an eventual rescue would become a warlike undertaking.

Today he spoke with ham operator América—PY5AEV—who is famous in the four corners of the world and always so attentive. Current position, verified by Orbicomm and Amyr's GPS: 60°S – 99°6W. (Hurray! Finally down to two digits!).

I told him that because of weather forecasts, the best thing would be for him to climb up to latitude 58°S to catch favorable winds to the Peninsula. He said that climbing two degrees is out of the question because it is too much distance. He will remain along 60°S, even if he runs the risk of headwinds.

In the evening, we enjoyed the visit of Gerard, Margi Moss, and Rafiki, their Great Dane. It was a party, especially for the twins because of the huge and friendly bow-wow. The Blonde says "good dog, good dog", and pets him. The Brunette, who wants to avoid risk at all cost, grabs the Blonde's hand and rubs it on the dog's coat, saying, "Stay, good dog!" We all laugh.

01/26

Gerard, Margi, and Rafiki have already gone. They continue their trip to Bolivia. Though the couple crossed the Americas, as well as the entire planet, in an Embraer single-engine plane, this time the trip is more conventional: vacation in Bolivia in a Land Rover. (I thanked them for the invitation, and I really would have liked to join them, but the way my life has been going lately . . .).

Ham radio operator Lopes—PY2SM—made contact and phone patched me to Amyr. He said my weather forecasts had come true.

Position: 59°S—94°1'W. I again told Amyr that the ideal thing to do would be to climb north-northwest about 65 miles, and that another low is shaping up along 55°S, behind him, bringing high waves. Temperature is –4°C, and will drop further, to –8°C, with conditions only improving after 01/30.

01/27

Today he called, in a bad mood. He said he is running into strong winds, about fifty knots (and I do not believe they are very favorable), and that he had somehow "blown out" the sail. Current position: 60°88'51"S—88°49'W. I felt that he was tense, and he insisted he would not climb northward because he had drawn a rhumb line for the Peninsula, and that he would not leave that course (regardless of the winds). I felt that he is dying to get there, especially when he asked me to tell him about the twins. I told him they are beginning to form sentences. This evening I gave a telephone interview to the University of São Carlos radio station, during my meteorology class. Estimated time of arrival at the Peninsula: next Tuesday. Let's hope he gets there soon!

01/28

Current position: 60°6'S—84°W. The low pressure system that brought yesterday's bad weather has passed, and he said it is unbelievably warm today: 7°C. He took advantage of the good weather and fixed the sail that tore yesterday. It seems that the mood on board has improved, especially now that there are only nine hundred miles to go before reaching Dorian Bay.

01/29

I spoke with Amyr. He seemed to be very homesick. He said he can't wait to sleep in a bed that doesn't move, and that the humidity on the boat is at 95%. Everything is getting damp on board.

He said the latest low pressure system hit 968 millibars, and that today, finally, he had no wind (eight-knot gusts). He was able to sew the sail that tore during the bad weather, though because the fabric is so thick, it was difficult. He plans to improve on the repair once he stops.

He is moving along at a fast clip, but he is cautious to ensure his arrival. He has been covering five degrees per day (excellent).

Fuel situation: six hundred liters. Enough to finish the voyage. I tell him about the invitation extended by the Brazilian Navy, to attend the 15th anniversary party at the Brazilian base on Antarctica, to be held on January 6, next Saturday. He will be on the Peninsula, however, besides the fact that he is dreaming of dropping anchor soon, the base is a little ways off the course he plans to take. The Brazilian base is on an unsheltered island and, with the daily weather forecasts he's been receiving, Amyr is worried about placing the boat at risk (there is some history of other sailboats and ships having problems around there).

He is at the mouth of the Weddell Sea, the exit point for many icebergs. While we were talking, a surprise: a beautiful rainbow appeared in front of the boat, which left him speechless for a few moments. It was 5:29 p.m. local time, 8:29 p.m. here in Brazil. I joked with him, saying that, as an event-producer, I had ordered that rainbow as a gift for him.

He sent a huge hug to all the people at Iridium, whose work allows us to remain close to each other at all times. I thanked the group of ham operators that provide us with unforgettable contacts, too.

01/31 to 02/05
Dorian Bay

Our communication was excellent. He is in a great mood. He has almost made it to the Peninsula. The seas are flat-calm. Current position: 61°46'S—69°13'W. He is 210 miles from Anvers Island.

The sailboat KOTIC is on its way back to Tierra del Fuego, because this absolute calm on the Peninsula is a harbinger of bad weather. Too bad. . . . They missed each other by a mere two days. He made arrangements with Júlio to swing by the base at Port Lockroy to pick up my gifts.

Time zone: plus two hours.

I think Amyr wants to go by the Brazilian base, but he will arrive there after the anniversary celebration.

Weather forecast I sent to Amyr's pager:

February 1 — 0 GMT 10 knots NW, smooth seas, –4°C.

February 2 — 0 GMT 20 knots NE, smooth seas, –4°C.

February 3 — 0 GMT 10 knots W, smooth seas, –4°C.

February 4 — 0 GMT 20–30 knots S, waves 25 feet, –8°C.

February 5 — 0 GMT 20–30 knots S, waves 25–30 feet, –12°C.

Not much farther to go before you get to enjoy your hard-earned rest. We are rooting for you. Good luck. Kisses from your favorite Marina.

02/02

What a coincidence. February 2, *Iemanjá* Day! Exactly eight years since PARATII left Dorian Bay, in 1991. Amyr returns to the place where he hibernated for eight months.

The last ten hours have been tense. Amyr has been every anxious to get there soon. The sun was shining and the sea was oily-slick until just before entering the channel. A 30- to

35-knot wind kicked up and created quite a stir, making the arrival a bit turbulent.

It began snowing heavily and visibility dropped significantly. He saw an orange fender up ahead, adrift. Just as the bow was about to pass by the fender, he began to think about how nice it would be to have a big fender like that on the boat. So he fished it up onto the bow. Ice made his approach difficult. He said several of the chunks got "painted red" as PARATII scraped by them on her way in.

At 19:27 (local) the anchor touched bottom. Only then did Amyr feel he had truly arrived in Dorian Bay.

The wind was blowing hard but, unbelievably, agreed to a five-minute truce just as he was ready to drop the anchor, which helped a lot. He dispatched the anchor quickly. He went ashore to tie her lines to rocks, and saw PARATII sitting just one hundred meters from where she had anchored through the winter years before. After 72 days without stepping ashore, exposed to the strongest winds on the planet, I asked him what he most wished for at that moment. He said that what he wanted more than anything else at that moment was to "turn on the heater."

02/03

Amyr was very happy. I believe that he feels "at home" in Dorian Bay. He said one of the first things he did was to take the dinghy over to Port Lockroy. This was not what one would call a safe stroll, because the winds were stiff, the sea was not calm, and there were walls of ice along the way.

To illustrate the low visibility, one of the highest peaks on the Antarctic Peninsula is on Anvers Island, right in front of the bay where PARATII was lying at anchor. Incredible as it might seem, even twenty-four hours after anchoring, Amyr has still not seen it.

"The landscape here is gray . . . very foggy. It is snowing heavily and the temperature is 0°C. The only things that stand out are the black-rock beach, the penguins, and the infinite shades of blue in the ice chunks passing by."

He is still getting himself organized. He has already picked up the surprise suitcase I put together for him. He said he was glad to see the present we sent him, but that he had not opened it yet.

The telephone here at home rang again. It was him. The first thing I heard was, "The Blonde's hair has grown!" (her hair had been really short when he left, and now she is sporting little curls).

I had sent photos taken of the twins at Christmas, so he could see how much they had grown. Their hands grew, too. "They look like adult hands!" A mini cassette recorder with their voices. I had no idea they could say all that! I didn't listen to all of it because I want to save it for tomorrow." The men's magazine. "Now, that's weird. You know, it was interesting to see that magazine and know that my wife was the one that sent it to me!"

The good news I gave him today was that it was the girls' first day of school. They loved it. They adapted much more easily than we had anticipated. In the recreation room there was an enormous fur seal (almost life-size), which they immediately identified. He had another of his silent spells, a temporary "moment of silence" during which he could not find words as he tried to grasp the fact that the girls are growing so fast and already in school.

02/04

Radio contact with Amyr was fun.

He said that he dedicated the day to housecleaning. He began by washing all of his clothes, and ended by taking a bath. (Now that is what I call housecleaning!)

While we were talking he told me he had just run off a leopard seal that was trying to chew on the rubber dinghy, and that the penguins around him were being very noisy. During the day he spotted two ships passing through Dorian Bay, but neither ship stopped. Unfortunately, his heater is not working very well.

"I met two guys who are trying to climb the highest peak on the Antarctic Peninsula, 9,200 feet. Today the skies cleared. The mountain is right in front of me here, and I was able to see the summit. But with this weather forecast, I will tell them they should begin their climb in four days."

"When I get back, remind me to tell how, unbelievably, the boat's engine started on a clutch-pop!

"Port Lockroy's delicious Marilyn Monroe is still there.

"Marina, give each of the girls a kiss."

Tonight, Lopes and Laslo arranged a phone patch between Amyr and Pedrinho Albuquerque. It was a total surprise for the kid, and the funniest thing about it is that I think he still wonders if it was truly Amyr and whether he was really calling "from PARATII straight from Dorian Bay."

02/05

Today we gave a live interview on Eldorado radio, on the Gioconda Bordon's show— Amyr, Hermann, and I. It was weird to talk with Amyr through the Iridium phone for 45 minutes, aware that so many people were listening in on our conversation. He spent the day organizing the boat, washing clothes, making minor repairs.

For dinner he had the friendly company of two Australians who will attempt to scale the highest summit in the region, on Anvers Island, directly in front of Dorian Bay. For as long as the weather remains poor, they are staying in a boat near the bay. Amyr said the Dutch cheese they brought was delicious! I gave him the weather forecast for the next four days, sent to his pager. I told him that because he is in the center of a high pressure area, the weather is good where he is, but it is running wild all around the Peninsula.

I am still unable to give him news about the sailboat WINSTON CHURCHILL, which was in the Sydney-Hobart Race, as he requested so he can ease the concerns of the gentleman who handles mail at Port Lockroy. I am awaiting news from Nysse Arruda, of Lisbon (she is always on top of these nautical matters).

02/07 to 02/13
DORIAN BAY AND THE BRAZILIAN BASE

02/07

A Swedish ship anchored near PARATII and invited Amyr to come aboard. He was warmly received and said what he liked best was the ship's sauna.

When he returned to PARATII they gave him a box of fruits and vegetables, which were a huge hit.

02/08

I thought his voice sounded unusually discouraged. He said he was feeling very tired. He spent the day fixing things, repairing the sails and, because they are so heavy, they had given him quite a workout.

The day was beautiful, with winds at six knots.

He has not heard anything from the Australian mountain climbers. He was concerned. He thinks their battery must have no power.

News: "It is incredible how worn out my foul-weather gear is. Not to mention my boots. They are turning into "blue galoshes," no longer "pairs of boots."

From school: the Blonde drank the Brunette's juice and ate her cookies. To get even, the Brunette ate her own sandwich, and then proceeded to eat the Blonde's sandwich, too.

02/09

Amyr called just as I was at the supermarket. I asked him if he would like me to buy something for him. He answered, "Wow! Potatoes!"

He was leaving Dorian Bay, headed for Deception Island. He left today and was happy because he had seen the first sailboat since he left Paraty. The Italian sailboat passed close by, about fifteen meters from him. The helmsman, Giorgio, recognized PARATII and Amyr, and called out his name. He spoke Portuguese. He said he had been to Paraty a few times. I think it will be another sleepless night.

At the end, he sent a kiss to each of the twins.

02/10

8:30 p.m. — Amyr is moored at the Brazilian base.

I imagine he is in a tough situation.

He took advantage of the favorable winds and, considering the bad-weather forecast, decided to head straight for the base, without anchoring at Deception Island.

We are at home.

Having twins is really interesting. What I have noticed is that children begin to play together at about two years of age. Today, for the first time the girls played a game together. Holding hands, they danced in circles repeatedly, until finally they shouted "Meow!"

Mom, for her part (as all moms should), danced alongside, feeling silly with joy as she watched this act of "human evolution."

I received Nysse Arruda's anxiously-awaited e-mail about the WINSTON CHURCHILL, which had participated in the Sydney-Hobart Race. Amyr wanted to ease the worries of the gentleman who handles mail at Port Lockroy, who had become friends with the crew. However, the news that arrived was not good at all.

Nysse's message said:

"On December 27, in the middle of the storm that covered the southern region near Australia and Tasmania, skipper Richard Winning sent out a Mayday and ordered everyone to abandon the boat because the hull had been seriously and irreversibly compromised. The crew of nine men divided into two boats and drifted out of each other's sight. For 24 hours the boats repeatedly capsized in the thirty-foot waves. At 9:00 p.m. on December 28, the second boat was found 60 miles from the place it had separated from the sailboat. Instead of five men, it was only carrying two, who were picked up by the frigate NEWCASTLE.

"The yacht SAYONARA, commanded by New Zealand's famous skipper, Chris Dickson, won the race, undamaged by the weather that decimated the fleet behind her.

"Six died and more than sixty boats withdrew during the first 24 hours of the race."

02/11

After sailing for 37 hours, carefully avoiding icebergs along the way, Amyr was very tense. Not surprising. From the outset of the voyage he was concerned with anchoring at the Brazilian base.

Today he was there, talking with terra firma, when he heard someone say that the anchor was dragging.

The 50-knot winds from Drake Passage hit there, causing a local 45-knot wind. It was sudden.

PARATII sailed away on her own. The base staff jumped into action to help Amyr. It was a mad race to reach her at sea, fighting the waves, the wind, and the torrential rain.

Summarizing what no one can tell better than he can: he got more drenched while rescuing the boat than he had in the entire voyage.

The twins were beautiful today, dressed as little clowns for their first-ever Carnival party. The party was held at their school. The best part was seeing them wearing their cardboard masks.

I sent Amyr the weather forecast for the Peninsula and Drake Passage for the next three days.

02/13

I began today's radio communication asking him how the karaoke organized at the Brazilian base for Carnival had gone (I was joking, because I know he doesn't like this sort of thing). He answered that the group's party was nice, but that he was unable to enjoy it.

He said the folks at the base were untiring in attending to him, including Commander Aquino, who spared no effort to lend whatever support was needed during Amyr's three days at the base (he doesn't stop praising the Proantar staff's goodwill and courage, noting that this mad rescue they had engaged in was just par for the course for them). Unfortunately, his stay was exhausting. The bad weather lasted all night long, forcing him to attempt to anchor fourteen times, facing mud up to his neck on the anchor chain, soaking clothes, and cold. The motor ran all night long, and the radar sounded at the passing chunks of ice, so Amyr did not get a chance to close his eyes even for one minute.

Today, Amyr left the Brazilian base. Next stop: South Georgia Island. Current position: 62°S— 58°W.

He should pass Elephant Island tonight, taking a more northerly course in order to make the most of favorable winds that should be blowing for the next three days, along 57°S.

02/14 to 02/20
HEADED FOR SOUTH GEORGIA ISLAND

02/14

Position: 59°40'S—54°37'W. Wind: WNE, 25–30 knots.

Eighty-four days have passed since Amyr began his Antarctic circumnavigation.

Today he is in the Drake Passage, heading north to meet favorable winds that should come in at about 58° or 57°S beginning tomorrow.

He remembered with clarity the most difficult situation he had encountered at the base:

"With wind gusts that sometimes reached 60 knots, making the sea white, I saw PARATII sailing away alone on the high seas. She was leaving, even with two anchors dropped. The mast's wing profile gave her all the sail area she needed."

He said he was still amazed. The British anchor he had used, considered to be the best in the world, with a lifetime warranty, had bent and exposed a sharp tip that later would damage the deck.

02/15

11:00 a.m Brasilia time. Position: 58°22'S—52°28'W. Temperature rising: 2°C. Water: 4.4°C. Interior of PARATII: 8°C.

Amyr said that Ricardo from the Brazilian base was extremely gracious to him. He gave Amyr some marine lubricants and, when he was departing, some fresh free-range eggs. Amyr is getting anxious to arrive at South Georgia and end his voyage. He also says that life at sea is a lot easier than life on land.

I asked him if he was putting his video equipment to good use. He said, no. That, incredibly, the tape collects condensation.

8:00 p.m. Brasilia time. Position: 57°37'S—51°7'W. Calm seas—the barometer is the same as it was this morning. The wind stiffened to thirty knots. Heading: 40°.

He is passing the Antarctic Convergence Line, so water temperatures are at 5°C. Estimate arrival on South Georgia Island: four days.

He said PARATII is closer and closer to being shipshape.

Strange: it smells like oysters in the forepeak because of the more than four hundred meters of wet and muddy anchor rode.

02/16

Position: 55°59'S—47°23'W. He just passed the latitude of Cape Horn. He is in the Scotia Sea, three hundred miles from Bird Island, beating upwind at seven knots. Average made good: 150 to 160 miles per day. Wind: thirty knots. Ten-foot waves, choppy seas.

Nearest land: Orkney Islands.

Official announcement: The sailboat PARATII has just completed 360 degrees around the earth! (he still needs to close out his route).

The twins, Grandma, and I went to the Carnival matinee dance.

02/17

My birthday. I am surprised he remembered, but Amyr calls me by phone to send me a birthday kiss. It is wonderful to hear his voice as he declares his love for me on this special day, even being so far from home.

Wind on Scotia Sea: 10–15 knots. Waves: small, ten feet. Temperature: 6°C. Course: north side of South Georgia Island.

Only 135 miles to go to complete the 360-degree Antarctic circumnavigation.

02/18

I heard Amyr's voice on the phone. He said he'd had a big scare today. He was inside PARATII, rounding the north side of South Georgia Island, heading for the same pier from which he had departed, when the boat suffered a knockdown, burying the mast in the water. The doors jammed. Though he wanted to rush and recover from the knockdown, he was unable to open the doors.

"Suddenly, one of those huge waves that were coming in 100-yard increments laid PARATII over on her side. The waves looked like walls of water. There I was, imprisoned in the boat, struggling to get out." The fifty-knot winds had occurred suddenly, and were not in the weather forecast at all.

I returned to the computer and double-checked and

checked again. There were no indications of fifty-knot winds in today's forecast for that region—nor for tomorrow.

He saw a dark spot a long way off. It was the island.

I was relieved when he realized it was not the island after all, but a ship having a more difficult time than PARATII, struggling to plow through the wind and waves. It looked like a test of skill, as if destiny wanted to test Amyr to see if he has what it takes to complete the challenge.

He is sailing cautiously. He hopes to tie up at the pier tomorrow morning, thus completing his circumnavigation.

02/19

The phone rang. It was 6:23 a.m. Amyr gave me the good news. He was entering the bay:

"Everything is fine. Now, that is. But you have no idea what a tight spot I just came through. . . . At the very moment I needed the engine, can you believe it? It wouldn't start. I went up on deck. Everything was wet. When the boat got knocked down, water came in through the daily tank intake and the engine froze. Thank goodness that is all it was. I bled the engine and it started normally. These trips are like this; you have to be alert until the very end."

I asked him what he could see.

"It is 6:36 a.m. I am entering Cumberland Bay. Deep inside the bay are two glaciers. Up front, there is another bay called Nordenskjold Glacier. The glacier is huge, huge, huge. A hole to the right of it is Grytviken Bay. The nearest mountains are black, and the backdrop mountains are white, with snowy peaks like the Alps. The water here is 4.4°C. It is daybreak . . . it is a very pretty day here.

"Oops! There is a chunk of ice right on PARATII's bow. It is so transparent I didn't even see it. There . . . I got around it.

"I am going to sign off. . . . Marina, you have no idea how much this moment means to me, what it means to enter through the same little slip of water I departed from when I left.

"Seventy-seven days sailing. Eighty-eight if we include the days at Dorian Bay (six days) and at the Brazilian base (three days). I added three days to my voyage just to reach those stopovers. It was faster than I thought it would be."

8:00 a.m. "I was looking for Harold, but he wasn't here because he is sick in bed on his boat. Hedel helped me tie up, and it was she who cast the lines when I left, too. This means a lot to me. This is a wonderful anchorage. I am tied up at the same pier I was earlier! I cannot believe this! It feels as if I was here only yesterday. It doesn't feel as if I have even been on a voyage!

"I would never make this trip again alone. Perhaps with a group of friends. I wanted you to be the first person to hear that I had arrived. Go to the girls' room and give each of them a kiss for me. A big kiss. I love you. Thank you for everything."

I said, "Congratulations, Amyr. We are proud of you. Now you just need to make it back home!"

I was so happy that I picked each of the girls up, one at a time, and played "airplane" with them (the game children love and mothers hate!).

I am enjoying describing Amyr's arrival, but I have to take the girls to school.

02/20

"I miss you, Marina! Watching PARATII tied up in this bay, I have the strange feeling that I never went on a voyage at all. Like I never left this place. As soon as I arrived I searched for

Harold, but it was Hedel, his wife, who helped me with the lines. They both cast my lines when I left. This couple is the only witness to my voyage. It was important that Hedel helped me tie up the boat. This has great meaning for sailors. She is a German woman, very friendly and funny.

"As soon as I arrived I opened the bottle of champagne (the one you gave me) and served up two cups, one for you and one for me.

"I am going to take advantage of the sunshine to take a bath on PARATII. Can you believe it is nice enough to just need a T-shirt? I want to take out everything that is salty so it can dry out. My overalls are filthy with diesel. I plan to wash all my clothes in the creek. The most important thing for me to do now is to put the boat in order.

"Good news: PARATII's heater is working again! It is heating the boat beautifully with the diesel fuel the guys gave me at the Brazilian base.

"Yesterday I ate penne with salmon and the bread the Brazilians gave me at the base. Toasted, with olive oil, it tasted fresh!

"Tomorrow's menu has been decided: spaghetti with cheese sauce. These menus of Takako's are marvelous."

As we do almost every night, our communications are by ham radio. Laslo arranges a phone patch. Tonight there were propagation problems, but despite all the static and noise, I heard him say one of the sweetest things he has said on the whole trip:

"The night is dark and the sea is absolutely flat—a mirror. The sea reflects the stars. It is so pretty! Too bad you aren't here. Marina, I dedicate this dark and starry night to you.

"Give each of the girls a kiss."

02/21 to 03/02
SOUTH GEORGIA ISLAND

02/21

I began by congratulating him on his skill in concluding yet another project. That we are happy and look forward to his return home.

He said he had decided to return to Brazil carrying only emergency water, trying to lighten the boat as much as possible given that the trip home is a tough one. He will most likely run into unfavorable wind.

"I plan to draw a line straight northward. I believe it should be about a 20-day sail. I could draw an arc toward Africa, but I prefer to head to Brazil. In fact, I hope not to have to go to Africa. I plan to sail through the center of the anticyclone.

"It was rainy this morning, but the sun came out in the afternoon. I washed all my clothes and almost froze my fingers off. Everything is squared away on the boat. Now I just need to shave.

"Instead of getting around by boat, I prefer to walk around the mountains around here. I have some gear with me.

"I noticed something interesting: when the wind is stronger, you can hear the tin roofs rattling atop the old abandoned houses. I will never forget that sound.

"Everything is cool. Today, a very famous boat came in. It belongs to a couple who was married here. They even imported a bishop from England and, while I was sailing around Antarctica, they were married in a pretty church here, which Harold restored.

"See you tomorrow. Kisses to the girls!"

02/24

Amyr said, "I cannot stand still, even here in Paradise!"

He is helping Harold dig ditches to make a sewage line for the South Georgia Island Museum, so he is working hard, breaking rocks down there.

He said he thinks he has lost some weight. He hasn't always had the time to eat well. Hedel thinks his legs are skinnier than they were when he started the voyage.

He said two sailboats came. With the large low pressure system at Cape Horn, Amyr asked me to send the latest weather forecasts, so he can pass them on to the new arrivals. (I confirmed 50-knot winds again). I sent the forecasts to Amyr's pager.

He said that now that he has visited the mountains on the north side of the island, he wants to climb the southern mountains.

Complete success: the twins took *brigadeiros* from Grandma's birthday party in their lunch boxes. Their little friends were delighted to join in eating them at snack time.

Their latest thing is to keep begging me for Band Aids with cartoon figures on them!

02/25

Today we spoke by ham radio. It was raining so hard that the connection was terrible. But it was worth it just to hear him say that everything is fine. He copied me perfectly. So I told him news about the twins and sent him a kiss.

That is so cool that Júlio (of ABUTRE) is going there by ship to meet him. He really is a good buddy. In January, he had taken the suitcase full of surprises to Antarctica for Amyr, together with Oleg, Stickel, and others. He just returned one week ago and now, in a mere second, he packed his bags again and headed back down, this time on a ship chartered by *Quark*, along with Breno and Eduardo of *Conspiração*.

They will bring new photos of Amyr and I took advantage of the opportunity to send him recent photos of the twins, because he still has not seen them in their school uniforms or in their Carnival costumes. Together with these photographs I sent a cassette on which are recorded some of the phrases they now can say, with a cute card attached to the package.

03/02

Temperatures are unusually high for South Georgia (16°C). Amyr spends the days barefoot, in a T-shirt. As forecast, strong winds (60 knots) came in during the afternoon, then quickly subsided. This could happen again tomorrow.

Today, Amyr said he experienced something interesting when an airplane of the British Air Force flew over the island and dropped fifteen large packages, each weighing about 150 pounds. They dropped by parachute, by coincidence precisely where PARATII is tied up.

These were food items for a fifteen-person military contingent that lives on the other side of the island. Their purpose is to preserve England's sovereignty over South Georgia Island.

"I saw all those packages falling, held by parachutes, one of which did not open. Then, the military personnel showed up to gather the packages. The packaging is so effective that there were even fresh eggs dropping from the sky. Those fresh eggs became part of my daily meals, too.

"The couple who were here on their honeymoon left yesterday."

03/07 to 03/14
RETURN TO BRAZIL

03/07

This week was very busy down there. It began with the arrivals of Júlio, Eduardo, and Breno. As if made to order: the
skies were overcast but improved when they sailed out to take
photos. They only have two busy days to try to make the most
of their visit, hoping to record a little of everything there is
to see.

Amyr cast off from Grytviken yesterday at 9:00 a.m., with
his course set for Rio de Janeiro.

Estimate time of arrival: twenty-four days. Position:
51°45'S—31°39'W. Strong winds, 55 knots, Waves: sixteen
feet, Temperature: 0°C.

"Due to the strong wind and choppy seas, the anchor
slammed many times and came loose from the bow. It was a
huge job to recover it and put it back in its place. Now my
whole body is sore from the effort. I am worn out.

"I ran into a lot of ice coming from the glaciers. I tried to
gain distance from South Georgia as quickly as possible. A
weather window opened up, thanks to Marina's forecasts.
The waves are not very high, but the sea is still white with
foam from cross seas."

03/08

Finally, the wind offers a truce!

PARATII left Grytviken on Sunday at 9:00 a.m., heading
north. Then, ice made Amyr's life difficult.

The strong winds gave no quarter. They reached sixty
knots. Breaking waves and heavy seas caused him to go 40
hours without sleep, without eating, and without being able to

get up on deck. Amyr described the scene, telling that sheets of non-skid were coming unglued, with some sent flying.

Flying only the storm trysail since he left Grytviken, Amyr considered reducing sail, until he realized it was already reduced as much as possible. While he was making twelve knots under the trysail, the anchor managed to break loose from the bow pulpit, causing huge problems.

He said he spent more than an hour half lying off the boat, getting slammed by cold waves and wind. He had no choice. He had to secure the 100-pound anchor to prevent it from dragging or ripping the hull. Thank goodness PARATII is not a fiberglass boat! After great effort, he was able to secure the anchor. He was shouting as he pulled the chain. He called home. He wanted me to tell him some cute story about the twins, just to get his mind off the business he had just been involved in. I told him that the forecast for tomorrow was for the wind to let up. He responded, "Poor PARATII, she is suffering so much. Do you think she'll withstand this wind until tomorrow?"

03/09

At 7:00 a.m. the phone rang.

Finally, the winds had died down some, to twenty knots. Finally, he was able to go below to eat. He engaged the autopilot and took a muscle relaxant; he was aching all over.

Here at home, we were greatly relieved to know that the gale had passed, and even happier to see that the center of the low pressure system had moved farther away from PARATII. That means Amyr should arrive home earlier than expected!

9:00 p.m. Everything is under control now. Position: 47°38'S—34°57'W.

He is 414 miles north of South Georgia. Headwinds, weak, ten to fifteen knots. Note of interest: He noticed a seal following PARATII, 230 miles north of South Georgia.

Celebration on board: Amyr is celebrating having climbed to 47°S. After almost five months, water temperatures are over 10°C.

03/11

Amyr called in the morning. He was very happy. The sea and wind were calm.

"A large pod of dolphins, dozens, maybe hundreds, is swimming around PARATII. The skies are partially overcast and there is a single ray of sunshine illuminating the dolphins. They are playing. There are two species: blue-silver and others that have a black spot on their backs. Imagine the scene . . ."

At the end of the afternoon, the phone rang again. He was in a terrible mood, very upset with a startling wind. After hovering around eighteen knots, a sudden gust of over 50 knots kicked up. After forty minutes, he realized this was not a mere gust, but that the winds had changed for real.

"What a scare! I was on deck with the wind hit. I surfed on my stomach, inch-worming across the deck to find a hand-hold. Marina, I almost went missing!"

He asked where the center of the depression was. I checked quickly. Unfortunately, the simplified weather program I am using does not give precise coordinates. I had to contact the Navy weather service to get that data.

Position: 45°S—34°W. Center of the low pressure system: 49°S—34°W, moving SW. It had already passed.

Good news: as of tomorrow, winds will be weaker. Bad news: I had to tell Amyr that winds will not let up until tomorrow.

03/12

After the blackout in central/south Brazil, electricity is back on. I breathed a sigh of relief when the phone rang and I saw it was him calling. For the third time since entering the Atlantic Ocean he has run into winds above 55 knots. In the Atlantic Ocean, waves are not as large as they are in the Indian and Pacific Oceans. But the wind surprised us.

"I have never gotten as wet as I have here in the Atlantic. Yesterday even my bones got wet. I changed clothes twice. Last night, as I was in the head changing into my third set of dry clothes, I heard a strange noise. I thought it must be the anchor that had come loose again. I decided to take a slight peak, so I opened the bow porthole—just a sliver enough to see with one eye. I think the noise must have been Neptune knocking, holding a bucket in the other hand. An entire wave came in through that porthole, flooding me and the head."

03/13

"Today, a day filled with sunshine, I saw something unusual. A group of small seagulls, about thirty, with black heads and white necks, started circling PARATII, playing like this: they flew around the boat, landed on the water just ahead of us, and then waited until we passed, almost touching them . . ."

It was interesting because Amyr was concerned with hitting them, and sometimes he tried to shoo them away, but they had their game to play!

"It seems as if the boat is going to run right over them. As the boat passes they take flight and settle ahead once again, waiting for PARATII to pass again. They are organized into three rows. (This lasted into the next day.)

"Look over there . . . the last albatross. No, the last three! One is very large, the oldest, and two smaller ones. The larger one must have about a three-meter wingspan, the smaller ones about two and a half meters. They are marvelous. This is the Queen Species of the bird world. They look like American bombers, with their wings slanted downward and their necks drawn in."

03/14

The seagulls continued to fly around the boat, playing their game.

Another day of sunshine, with water temperatures at an impressive 22°C. The water is warmer than the air, and warmer than the bath water, too.

It's wonderful not to have to turn on the heater anymore!

"I am going to square away the boat and put by clothes out to dry."

Good news! The weather forecast is for favorable winds, which should speed up his arrival even more.

03/20 to 03/29
PARATY, BRAZIL

03/20

The twins and I went to Paraty. According to Amyr's contacts and the Orbicomm's latest positions, he should arrive sometime between Saturday night and Sunday morning.

03/21

8:45 a.m. Spectacular sunny morning in Jurumirim (Paraty).

In the sand on the beach we watched boats coming in to witness Amyr's arrival. Among them, far off, a red sailboat, arriving . . . it's PARATII!

All three of us were playing on the beach and, as the boat drew closer, I called the girls, and showed them that Daddy was arriving.

They watched silently, mute, and that is how they remained, with their eyes fixed on the red sailboat.

Soon, unable to contain my own emotions, I picked them up and held them.

Amyr was arriving. Six long months away from our eyes, away from our home.

I did not feel alone for a single minute, because we were close throughout the entire time. But seeing the sailboat arrive, and Amyr standing on deck . . . I felt, for just a second, what a momentous voyage he had undertaken and was ending at that moment.

To be the first man to circumnavigate the frozen continent . . . and to have done it "alone!" It's not just anyone who can make a trip like that.

He had my support from land, holding things under control at home. I think I am his greatest motivator.

A little later, as we ate breakfast as a family, the Blonde could not even move, she was so excited. She didn't even blink as she sat next to her father.

03/22

A fun day.

When he got out of bed, after his first night home, Amyr bumped into the door. I laughed and asked what had happened. He said that when he stepped on land, he had not felt the ground move. He said it was strange to walk through a door that wasn't leaning sideways.

03/24

We were asleep at the little house in Jurumirim when they invaded PARATII. Amyr noticed and thought it strange that he couldn't see the two gas tanks that had made it around the world with him. During the night someone had broken into the boat and stolen some of its equipment, including the tape recordings, photos, and videos he had taken along the journey.

03/25

The twins' birthday, celebrated at water's edge, with flags, cake, the works . . . (and Daddy was there!).

03/29

Good news: the Mayor's office called today to tell us they had recovered some of the stolen equipment, but I don't think the tape recordings and images will ever be recovered.

RECOMMENDED READING

ALEXANDER, Caroline. *The Endurance—Shackleton's Legendary Antarctic Expedition.* New York, NY: Knopf. 1998

AMUNDSEN, Roald. *The South Pole.* London: C. Hurst and Company. 1978

Antarctica, Great Stories from the Frozen Continent. Pleasantville, NY: Reader's Digest. 1985

Antarctic Pilot, The N.P.9. Hydrographer of the Navy. United Kingdom. 1974

BARTON, Humphrey. *Atlantic Adventurers: Voyages in Small Craft.* New York: J. de Graff. 1962

BONINGTON, Chris. *Quest for Adventure: Ultimate Feats of Modern Exploration.* Washington, DC: National Geographic. 2000

BULLIMORE, Tony. *Saved: the Extraordinary Tale of Survival and Rescue in the Southern Ocean.* London: Little Brown and Company. 1997

CARR, Tim and Pauline. *Antarctic Oasis: Under the Spell of South Georgia.* New York, NY: W.W. Norton and Company. 1998

CHERRY-GARRARD, Apsley. *The Worst Journey in the World.* Washington, DC: National Geographic. 2002

CLARK, Gerry. *The Totorore Voyage: an Antarctic Adventure.* London: Century Hutchinson. 1988

FISHER, James and Margery. *Shackleton.* Boston, MA: Houghton Mifflin. 1958

HARRISON, Peter. *Seabirds: An Identification Guide.* Boston, MA: Houghton Mifflin. 1991

HEADLAND, Robert K. *The Island of South Georgia.* New York, NY: Cambridge University Press. 1992

HUNTFORD, Roland and Paul Theroux. *The Last Place on Earth*. Modern Library. 1999

HUNTFORD, Roland. *Shackleton*. London: Hodder and Stoughton. 1985

LANSING, Alfred. *Endurance: Shackleton's Incredible Voyage*. New York, NY: McGraw-Hill Co. 1959

PALO JR., Haroldo. *Antártida—Expedições brasileiras*. Rio de Janeiro: Cor Ação Editora. 1989

PONCET, Sally. *Le Grand Hiver: DAMIEN II, Base Antarctique*. Paris: Arthaud.

WILSON, Edward, A. *Diary of the Terra Nova Expedition to the Antarctic 1910–1912*. Poole, Dorset: Blandford Press. 1972

WORSLEY, Frank A. *Shackleton's Boat Journey*. New York, NY: W.W. Norton and Company. 1998

Other books of interest from Sheridan House

SAILING ALONE AROUND THE WORLD
Joshua Slocum
"... an account of the first solo circumnavigation of the globe ... Slocum's writing is as elegant as his thirty-seven-foot sloop, *Spray*, whose crossing of the Atlantic he describes vividly." *The New Yorker*

THE LONG WAY
Bernard Moitessier
"Moitessier was the original mystical mariner. This account of his most legendary exploit, in which he blew off winning the 1969 singlehanded non stop Golden Globe round-the-world race so he could 'save his soul' in high southern latitudes, is a bible to ocean sailors with a metaphysical bent. His decision to quit the race and keep on sailing, in more ways than one, marks the point at which ocean racing and ocean cruising went their separate ways." *Cruising World*

CAPE HORN
THE LOGICAL ROUTE
Bernard Moitessier
An account of the Moitessiers' honeymoon trip from Europe to the islands of the Pacific and back along the "logical route" via Cape Horn, a path chosen for its speed, which took them through the Roaring Forties, iceberg territory and the relentless gale-force winds of higher latitudes.

"A true classic by and about one of cruising's best known authors."
Latitudes & Attitudes

MOITESSIER
Jean-Michael Barrault
"In this biography, Barrault succeeds in capturing a wanderer's life that encompassed the successes, failures and inconsequential doings left in the wake of a pelagic philosopher and free spirit" *Cruising World*

"Barrault's very personal portrait of his old friend is affectionate and honest." *SAIL*

"Great insight into a fascinating man." *Latitudes & Attitudes*

THROUGH THE LAND OF FIRE
FIFTY-SIX SOUTH
Ben Pester
"Tierra Del Fuego and Patagonia are some of the most exciting areas on this earth to cruise and the author takes you on an exciting voyage through the colorful and sometimes dangerous areas first sailed by Magellan. For some sailors this is the Holy Grail of sailing, so sit back and see why it is such an enticing mistress." *Latitudes & Attitudes*

America's Favorite Sailing Books
www.sheridanhouse.com

Other books of interest from Sheridan House

FURTHER OFFSHORE
Ed Mapes

This practical guide to offshore sailing will appeal to all those sailors who have honed their skills as day sailors, racers and coastal sailors and who are now planning to go further and become bluewater sailors. Captain Mapes takes us from practical and psychological preparation to equipping your boat, navigation skills, heavy weather and eventually landfall.

LAST GREAT ADVENTURE
WITH THE SEA MASTER FROM THE ANTARCTIC TO THE AMAZON
Sir Peter Blake

"This emotional book tracks . . . the outstanding yachtsman, adventurer and international sporting celebrity, on his final voyage."

Offshore Magazine

DO DOLPHINS EVER SLEEP
211 QUESTIONS AND ANSWERS ABOUT SHIPS, THE SKY, AND THE SEA
Pierre-Yves and Sally Bely

"With topics covering astronomy, biology, naval architecture and oceanography among others, this eclectic work, popularized with talent and very well illustrated, is accessible to all curious sailors. Indispensable aboard!"

Voiles Magazine

ATLANTIC CROSSINGS
A SAILOR'S GUIDE TO EUROPE AND BEYOND
Les Weatheritt

Covering prevailing winds and other seasonal considerations, the author not only deals with suitable starting points on the East coast but also covers in great detail the best and most popular destination sites in Europe. Several appendices provide additional useful information.

SALVAGE
Captain Ian Tew

The story covers the ten years Captain Ian Tew spent with Selco Salvage in Singapore and ranges from the UK coast to the South China Sea, from the Persian Gulf to the Southern Ocean. It involved performing salvage operations in storm force winds as well as in tropical calms. He packed more adventure into ten years than many see in a lifetime.

America's Favorite Sailing Books
www.sheridanhouse.com